LEADERSHIP 55
LESSONS IN SCHOOL LEADERSHIP

JOHN TOMSETT

Together we unlock every learner's unique potential

At Hachette Learning (formerly Hodder Education), there's one thing we're certain about. No two students learn the same way. That's why our approach to teaching begins by recognising the needs of individuals first.

Our mission is to allow every learner to fulfil their unique potential by empowering those who teach them. From our expert teaching and learning resources to our digital educational tools that make learning easier and more accessible for all, we provide solutions designed to maximise the impact of learning for every teacher, parent and student.

Aligned to our parent company, Hachette Livre, founded in 1826, we pride ourselves on being a learning solutions provider with a global footprint.

www.hachettelearning.com

Although every effort has been made to ensure that website addresses are correct at time of going to press, Hachette Learning cannot be held responsible for the content of any website mentioned in this book. It is sometimes possible to find a relocated web page by typing in the address of the home page for a website in the URL window of your browser.

Hachette UK's policy is to use papers that are natural, renewable and recyclable products and made from wood grown in well-managed forests and other controlled sources. The logging and manufacturing processes are expected to conform to the environmental regulations of the country of origin.

To order, please visit www.HachetteLearning.com or contact Customer Service at education@hachette.co.uk / +44 (0)1235 827827.

ISBN: 978 1 0360 1061 4

© John Tomsett 2025

First published in 2025 by
Hachette Learning (a trading division of Hodder & Stoughton Limited),
An Hachette UK Company
Carmelite House
50 Victoria Embankment
London EC4Y 0DZ
www.HachetteLearning.com

The authorised representative in the EEA is Hachette Ireland, 8 Castlecourt Centre, Dublin 15, D15 XTP3, Ireland (email: info@hbgi.ie)

Impression number   10 9 8 7 6 5 4 3 2 1
Year   2029 2028 2027 2026 2025

All rights reserved. Apart from any use permitted under UK copyright law, no part of this publication may be reproduced or transmitted in any form or by any means, electronic or mechanical, including photocopying and recording, or held within any information storage and retrieval system, without permission in writing from the publisher or under licence from the Copyright Licensing Agency Limited. Further details of such licences (for reprographic reproduction) may be obtained from the Copyright Licensing Agency Limited, www.cla.co.uk

Typeset in the UK.

Printed in the UK.

A catalogue record for this title is available from the British Library.

John Tomsett taught for 33 years in state schools and was a teaching secondary headteacher for 18 years. He writes a blog called *This Much I Know* and has written extensively about school leadership. He has published 13 books, including: *Love Over Fear: Creating a Culture for Truly Great Teaching*; *Putting Staff First: A Blueprint for Revitalising our Schools* (with Jonny Uttley); *Cognitive Apprenticeship in Action* (editor); *Huh: Curriculum conversations between subject and senior leaders*; *Primary Huh: Curriculum conversations with subject leaders in primary schools*; *Primary Huh 2: Primary curriculum leadership conversations*; *SEND Huh: Curriculum conversations with SEND leaders*; and *AP Huh: Curriculum conversations with alternative provision leaders* (all with Mary Myatt); *Truly Great Primary Teachers (and what we can learn from them)* and its sister book, *Truly Great Secondary Teachers (and what we can learn from them)*, and *Leadership 55: Lessons in School Leadership* with Haringey Education Partnership.

He maintains that the best thing for our students is that our teachers are happy, healthy, well-qualified, highly motivated, hard-working, well-trained experts. Consequently, he believes we should put staff first.

www.johntomsett.com
X: @johntomsett

This book is dedicated to all those working, day in, day out, with children in Haringey Education Partnership schools and whose unheralded moments of teaching and learning magic take place in the corners of their classrooms on cold, wet Thursday afternoons…

Contents

Preface by John Tomsett ix

Chapter 1 A conversation on leading HEP with James Page and
Fran Hargrove 1

Chapter 2 A conversation on assessment with Professor
Dylan Wiliam 9

Chapter 3 Leadership 55 wisdom – the essence of the
headteacher's job 21

Chapter 4 A conversation on SEND with Margaret Mulholland 23

Chapter 5 Leadership 55 wisdom – establishing your core purpose 39

Chapter 6 A conversation on leading writing with Alex Quigley 43

Chapter 7 Leadership 55 wisdom – teaching and learning 57

Chapter 8 A conversation on diversity with Bennie Kara 63

Chapter 9 Leadership 55 wisdom – being patient 73

Chapter 10 A conversation on instructional coaching with
Jim Knight 77

Chapter 11 Leadership 55 wisdom – understanding the finances 93

Chapter 12 A conversation on assessment with Professor
Becky Allen 97

Chapter 13 Leadership 55 wisdom – change management 101

Chapter 14 A conversation on Ofsted with Malcolm Willis 109

Chapter 15 Leadership 55 wisdom – coping with the loneliness 119

Chapter 16 A conversation on cognitive science with Jade Pearce 123

Chapter 17 Leadership 55 wisdom – the buck stops with you 135

Chapter 18 A conversation on unpacking oracy with Clare Sealy 139

Preface

Time is of the essence. Always. Especially if you're leading a school. So, when Heather De Silva, Haringey Education Partnership's indefatigable professional development lead asked me whether I'd like to host a live leadership webinar aimed at keeping HEP's busy school leaders up to date with the world of education, I agreed immediately.

To emphasise the lack of time in our lives, Heather suggested that each webinar be less than an hour long. She suggested we call it 'Leadership 55', as in 55 minutes long! It seemed like it might work. We might even abbreviate it to L55? What about a logo? How about if each episode includes an interview with a big player in the edu-world? We could ask some *grand fromages*, like Professors Dylan Wiliam and Becky Allen… The more we talked, the more enthused we became.

The thing is, when you get carried away with an idea, you can soon get blinded by your own enthusiasm. What seemed like the best idea in the world last evening on a Zoom call can appear incredibly prosaic when you run it by someone the next morning. Not so with Leadership 55. HEP's leadership team, James Page and Fran Hargrove, loved the idea and proposed they provide bite-sized updates on news from the DfE and Ofsted. Heather suggested I provided a five-minute wisdom-piece on something I had learned about leading schools.

So, with a germ of an idea and more front than Brighton and Hove put together, we approached some potential guests. I have learned over the years that the likes of Dylan Wiliam are just damned decent people who are always willing to help if they can. So, Dylan agreed to appear on our first episode of L55 with a brilliant piece on assessment. Becky Allen was next, with a counter-piece to Dylan's. Put the two episodes together and there's most of what you might need to know about assessment in schools.

When the guest interviews are bookended by James and Fran's DfE/Ofsted updates and my wisdom think-pieces, the webinars provide 55 minutes of concentrated usefulness. Over the past two years we have managed to enable our school leaders to hear from some of the best thinkers practising in education today, in a format that they can access easily in their busy lives.

The final proposal came from Heather. 'How about a book, John?' And, never backward in going forward, I approached John Catt Educational, who liked the sound of the idea and the names of the contributors we might include. So, huge thanks go to Alex at John Catt Educational for having faith in this project, as well as all those generous guests who have appeared on the L55 webinar. And it would be wrong not to acknowledge Luke Kemper, HEP's Lead for Insight and Intelligence, who has helped edit the interview transcripts.

It does seem right to have published the golden nuggets of the L55 webinars – material that has, until this point, only been accessed by the school leaders affiliated to HEP. Some of the thinking in the following pages is cutting-edge stuff – Alex Quigley on literacy… Margaret Mulholland on SEND… Bennie Kara on diversity – and this book brings such wisdom to a much wider audience.

One other thing… Your purchase of this book will contribute to HEP's charity, Horizons, which provides extracurricular opportunities for those children and young people for whom such opportunities are out of reach. Horizons' vision is that through equity of access to extracurricular activity, ALL children and young people in Haringey and Enfield will have the opportunity to fulfil their enormous potential.

There is never enough time. But, if you can, do find a few minutes – 55 if possible – to sit with this book and your brew of choice, and enjoy learning from some of the most insightful people working in education today.

John Tomsett, February 2025

Chapter 1
A conversation on leading HEP with James Page and Fran Hargrove

John Tomsett (JT): Where did HEP come from? What made HEP happen?

Fran Hargrove (FH): In 2016, Haringey faced a challenging period with intervention from the Department for Education. This was around the time of a significant shift towards forced academisation. Just before this, there had been considerable political tension surrounding one of the schools and its mandated conversion to an academy, which left many schools feeling vulnerable. Historically, Haringey has been a very collegial borough, where headteachers and schools work closely together. The area is relatively compact, with schools in close proximity to one another, fostering a long tradition of collaboration among headteachers and their institutions.

Back in the early 2000s, Haringey was at the forefront of 'Network Learning Communities', an initiative introduced by the DfE as part of their White Paper strategies. It focused on local collaboration and building a sense of place. The systems to support this were well established, and the local authority managed a fairly comprehensive school improvement service. However, as time went on, this service grew somewhat outdated and compliance-driven, especially as public sector cuts led to redundancies. Many individuals providing school improvement support had been in the local authority for a long time but lacked recent leadership experience or practical insights from time spent as headteachers or in school leadership roles.

At that point, a group of us – all headteachers – came together. I was part of this group, and we began to explore how we could channel our shared sense of moral purpose, a quality that is deeply ingrained in Haringey – a collective responsibility, if you will. There was a phrase that summed it up well: 'accountable for some and responsible for all'. That idea became the foundation of our approach.

As a group, we had reached the conclusion that we no longer wanted to delegate school improvement responsibilities to the local authority. The local authority was very supportive of this decision, as the political environment at the time was favourable toward such initiatives. Together, we set out to envision what an ideal school improvement model would look like if we managed it ourselves.

A steering group of headteachers was established to move this work forward, and I was honoured to be asked to lead it. I agreed, albeit somewhat reluctantly at first, and now it's become a real passion of mine, a very personal endeavour. We researched various school improvement models in different local authorities and looked at emerging education partnerships. We brought our findings back to the group of headteachers and began to have deep discussions about what mattered to us, about what school improvement should mean in our context.

We developed a model that centred on leadership, curriculum and pedagogy, analysing everything through these three pillars. Although school improvement partners were becoming less popular due to their inconsistent quality, we recognised the importance of such relationships.

We also discussed the 'glue' in the system – the sense of place, the importance of our community and our shared commitment to our children.

Through a series of steering group meetings, I presented various options to the group, asking questions like, 'Would you prefer this, or that?' This was around the time Mr Page joined us. If I remember correctly, that was back in 2017.

JT: James, how did you enter the scene?

James Page (JP): Before this, I was involved in different areas within the local authority – first in children's social care support, then adult social care. When Jon Abbey took on the director of children's services (DCS) role, he asked me and a colleague to jointly take on the assistant director (AD) role at the council. My main task was to get Haringey Education Partnership (HEP) set up while maintaining stability in the existing system. This gave me a clear, singular focus.

From the council side, I could bring together all the support we needed – funding, legal assistance, procurement and political backing. Working closely with Fran and the steering group of headteachers, I had significant leverage. I could return to the council and insist that HEP wouldn't succeed unless it met the needs and expectations of the headteachers. This gave me powerful tools to overcome many of the typical barriers and challenges within the local authority.

FH: Yes and, at that time, I said I wouldn't work for it, which, looking back, sounds a bit mad! The idea was for someone with formal qualifications to lead it. And, now, here we are.

JT: So this was very much a bottom-up initiative. There was a gap, a need, and the two of you stepped in to drive it forward. It launched in 2018. But how did you both transition from your previous roles to becoming part of HEP, rather than staying in your positions as a headteacher and an AD?

JP: We held a headteachers' conference in July 2018, with the goal of launching HEP by September 2018. At that point, we had a strong commitment from around 45 schools in Haringey, although it wasn't quite viable yet. The support largely came from primary schools, which had to unite to confirm that this was what they wanted. During that conference, we were still finalising applications for the improvement partners we hoped to bring on in September.

Just weeks before the summer holidays, we left that conference with commitments from about 60 schools in total. It was nearly a majority, although not every school in Haringey. Interestingly, we even had a couple of schools from Enfield joining us; they knew us and decided to come on board from the outset, albeit in a limited capacity. The level of uncertainty and risk was huge. Fran and I left our previous positions to take on the responsibility of running HEP.

JT: That was a major commitment. And the culture piece?

FH: Yes, that was the point where the culture was truly established. One of our non-negotiables was that nobody would be seconded or retain their local authority employment terms. This meant no transfer of teachers' pay, conditions or local government pensions. We are entirely independent, with our own pension and benefits structure. To join HEP, you had to leave behind that traditional security.

JT: That makes people sharper, doesn't it?

FH: Absolutely, it does. It makes you want to be fully invested in the job. Our timelines were incredibly tight. When I decided to do this, I had to resign from my previous role well before the official application for the position I wanted was even available. You have to be willing to take that leap. This commitment level is something that continually comes up when we talk to other education partnerships; they often ask us how we cultivated such a strong culture. I believe it came down to the urgency we faced. You had to want to be part of it for the right reasons.

JT: And what about the governance structure?

JP: Initially, we had a shadow board while we were designing HEP, which functioned as a decision-making body even though it had no legal standing until we officially incorporated the company. The board included the director of children's services, the lead member for children's services from the local authority and several headteachers. The current board structure includes three permanent positions: myself, the independent chair of the board, and the director of children's services.

Additionally, we have a rotating group of eight headteachers and chairs of governors who serve two-year terms. This set-up emphasises that HEP is led by schools and reflects true school ownership.

JT: So, you're structured as a limited company?

JP: Yes, exactly. The majority of our board members are headteachers and chairs of governors, which reinforces our accountability to them.

JT: Tell me about your moral purpose.

FH: It's like the idea of a broad and balanced curriculum – a very relevant concept. Our moral purpose is to ensure that the children we serve are at the centre of everything we do. We support them by working with leaders and teachers, essentially flipping the triangle so that children are at the top, with all our efforts directed upward toward them. In every decision we make, we ask ourselves how it will support the education and opportunities provided to these children. We're funded by public money to serve other people's children, so every pound spent must go toward improving their lives and choices.

JP: Exactly, and that moral purpose is also deeply embedded in how we've structured our operations. It's essential to our approach. We've always been clear with our schools: HEP is a single-tier membership organisation – you're either fully in, or you're not. This isn't a transactional service; it's a collective commitment to shared responsibility and accountability for our children. Our approach is rooted in knowing our schools, building long-term relationships through years of collaborative improvement, and striving for the best possible outcomes for the children we serve. It's never about selling more services.

JT: Back to 2018, you launched. Tell us about that first year.

FH: It was brilliant, absolutely brilliant, but also make or break. We had promised the world, and now we had to deliver. Headteachers are incredibly exacting and demanding, and there was a real sense of apprehension because we had a completely new team and no blueprint to follow. We needed to build the team, establish the culture and deliver excellence right from the start. It was intense but also exhilarating. There was a strong sense that there was nothing we couldn't achieve if we put our minds to it. We were agile, able to respond and make decisions quickly.

Thanks to the financial backing from the local authority, we had the resources to meet schools' needs promptly and make effective decisions.

JP: We did ask schools to invest significantly in membership, so the quality of what we delivered had to be exceptional. By the end of that first year, we had added about 15 to 20 more schools, and nearly every school in Haringey had joined us. We were also beginning to expand into Enfield, which allowed us to broaden our reach and impact.

FH: The improvement partners were essential to our success. We were meticulous in our recruitment, bringing in not just skilled individuals but people whose expertise aligned with our mission. We focused on creating a strong sense of identity for them, even though they were consultants. Their work has real significance. The feedback from headteachers and improvement partners has been incredibly positive. They serve as the primary connectors for HEP, brokering access to everything else we offer.

JT: What was your offer in that first year? Was it largely around school improvement partners?

JP: Predominantly, yes. There were data packs, a racial equity programme, the CPD programme, Network Learning Communities and governance support. We also had the headteacher hotline, which was essentially just Fran's mobile number.

JT: You mentioned the change in the Ofsted framework in 2019. How did that impact HEP?

JP: The new Ofsted framework was significant. We needed to grasp not only the language but also the underlying principles. We invited Christine Counsell to speak with our headteachers, which was transformative. She delved into why curriculum matters, advocating for a knowledge-rich curriculum, equity and high ambition. This discussion led to the launch of our Opening Worlds programme in 2019, though it was delayed by Covid. It helped us deepen our thinking and link cognitive science to curriculum and pedagogy. This experience showed us that we could operate at a high level and establish partnerships with national significance.

JT: Then Covid hit...

FH: Yes, Covid was a pivotal moment. Initially, we worried because we couldn't be in schools or run in-person training. But we adapted quickly, moving everything online. Heather De Silva, who led CPD, was instrumental in this transition. We brought in renowned speakers to present to our heads and schools and, by scheduling training at 4pm, we saw attendance soar, often reaching over a hundred participants. As a result, our staff and schools became more comprehensively trained than ever. Improvement partners also adapted, tackling challenging aspects of school improvement remotely. We served as a vital link between all departments in the local authority, helping to streamline support for schools. This period also gave rise to the HEP weekly Monday briefing, where we distilled important guidance for schools.

JP: There were two other crucial developments during this time. Schools sought out CPD resources and found value in Rosenshine's principles and Tom Sherrington's *WalkThrus*. We were at the forefront, purchasing subscriptions and integrating these resources across our network. This allowed us to solidify our focus on pedagogy, leadership and curriculum.

JT: Having both Counsell and Sherrington involved is significant.

JP: Absolutely. Their involvement enabled us to reinforce our approach to leadership, curriculum and pedagogy, allowing us to address issues through those perspectives. We also launched a charitable arm, Horizons, to support equitable access to extracurricular activities – a need we recognised when disparities in access became stark during home-schooling.

JT: What does success look like for you?

JP: Our top priority is outcomes for children. Achieving the London average for Key Stage 2 reading, writing and maths is an incredible accomplishment for Haringey, a borough that has historically ranked among the lowest three to five in London. We measure our success through these outcomes and the feedback from our annual survey with member schools. Our average rating from headteachers and chairs of governors is 9.1 out of 10, which shows that we're making a positive impact.

FH: For us, growth isn't about commercial expansion; it's about people seeking us out because they recognise the value we bring. That's humbling. Feedback from Ofsted also reflects our impact. Our focus is on building meaningful relationships and establishing a respected presence in the system, fully aware of the responsibility that entails. It's about our engagement with member schools and enriching the professional lives of those who work with us.

JT: Where are you heading next?

FH: We want to continue doing the right thing while staying stable and financially secure so that we can serve our member schools with excellence. We believe we have much to contribute in terms of place-based education.

JP: We're not an isolated entity. I'm currently chairing the London Boroughs Group Strategic Education Leads, which keeps us connected with the DfE and Ofsted regional directors. We're also collaborating with the Association of Education Partnerships and maintaining strong relationships with key figures in the education sector. Another priority is expanding Horizons, our charitable arm, to support equitable access to extracurricular activities. Our goal is to make a difference both inside and outside the classroom.

Chapter 2
A conversation on assessment with Professor Dylan Wiliam

John Tomsett (JT): I'm delighted to welcome Dylan to our webinar, our first Leadership 55 webinar. I've asked Dylan to talk about whole-school assessment. Over to you, Dylan.

Dylan Wiliam (DW): Thanks, John. Well, I think the first thing to say: I'm not going to tell you how to do whole-school assessment. I think what we've learned is that any school assessment system needs to take into account the local school context, but I think what might be helpful is for me to lay out a few principles that I found useful in thinking about assessment. So if you think about it, what I'm going to try to do is to help you think in a more productive, creative and critical way about assessments in your school. Then I think you can take your own purposes, your own needs into account, but it's just taking into account what we've learned in something like a hundred years of research on educational assessment. So the first thing to say is, well, what is an assessment?

I think the most helpful definition comes from Lee Cronbach, who over 50 years ago now said: an assessment is basically a procedure for drawing conclusions. We give students things to do. We look at what they did; we draw conclusions. If you think about it from that perspective, I think everything makes a lot more sense. There's no such thing as a valid test. A test can be valid for some purposes and not others.

Let me give you an example. Let's say I give a maths test to a group of students and they're all fluent readers, which is good because the test has quite a high reading demand. Most of the variation scores that I see will be caused by their differences in mathematics achievement. So, hopefully, students who are good at maths get high scores; students who are weak at maths get lower scores; that's helpful. If I give it to a more mixed group of students, then some of the variations in scores will be caused by differences in maths achievement, but some of the variation will be caused by reading ability, in which case I don't know how to interpret the scores. A high score means they're probably good at both, but a low score? Is that because they weren't able to read the question or was it because they didn't know the maths? So the crucial thing here – it's got a complicated psychological term but I'm not going to use that for a while – we want the differences in scores to represent the differences in the things we care about. The problem is sometimes test scores depend on things they shouldn't.

In history for example, we want test scores to reflect differences in historical ability. If we use essay questions, we may find that we're actually assessing language and handwriting skill and handwriting speed as much as anything else. So the first problem with assessments is sometimes scores depend on things they shouldn't, and that includes bias in teacher marking. One teacher is a lenient marker; one teacher is a severe marker. Your score should not depend on who does the marking. Your score should not depend on whether you're having a good day or a bad day. Your score should not depend on whether the particular choice of writing prompt, for example, was one that you had actually thought about recently. In a history exam, if you had revised the particular topics that came up on the essay questions, you will do well. If you revised different topics, you will do badly. The first problem: the complicated scientific term for this is 'construct-irrelevant variance'. I'll just unpack that a bit. Variation in scores is called 'variance' in statistics. We want the variation in scores to be relevant to the thing we're assessing, the construct. So if the variation in scores is caused by things that are irrelevant to the construct we're assessing, maths achievement for example, then we have construct-irrelevant variance. I think basically you capture all of that scientific idea in the idea of scores depending on things they shouldn't.

The opposite problem is the scores don't depend on things they should. So if I assess science entirely with a written test with no practical, two students with the same academic skills, but where one has a far higher mastery of practical skills than the other, will get the same score and that's not fair. The student who is actually better at some aspects of science, the practical aspect, should somehow have that additional expertise reflected in their scores. So those are the two main problems bedevilling assessment: scores depending on things they shouldn't; scores not depending on things they should. That then affects the conclusions we can draw. So I think the first step in thinking smartly about assessment is to say, 'There's no such thing as a valid assessment.' Describing an assessment as valid is like describing a rock as happy. It's what Gilbert Ryle called a 'category error'. A rock cannot be happy because happiness is not a property that rocks are capable of possessing. In the same way validity is not a property of tests. Validity is a property of conclusions and in a way that actually harkens back to the way we use the word 'valid' in ordinary language: a valid conclusion.

So the correct question to ask is not 'Is this a valid test?', but 'What conclusions can I draw when I see the test results?' When people ask me to validate a test I say, 'Tell me what you propose to conclude about these students from these test results and I will tell you whether that's warranted or not.' This is a real problem in all kinds of assessment used because we make assessments do double duty and it's perfectly understandable because assessments are expensive in terms of time. So why shouldn't we actually make an assessment serve as many different purposes as possible? For example, GCSEs used to be used just to certify students' ability to benefit from sixth-form study. A-levels used to be used solely to judge the suitability of a student for university education, but then we started using them as guides to the quality of a school, which is stupid because actually most of the variation in GCSE scores is not caused by the quality of education those students have received. It's caused by how much those students knew when they arrived at the school.

It's like regarding Great Ormond Street Hospital in London as a bad hospital because the mortality rates are higher than the average cottage hospital. Yes, because they take the sickest patients. In the health service it's widely agreed that you should never report mortality or morbidity stats. What you should do is talk about risk-adjusted mortality stats. So when you arrive in any hospital in England, your condition is assessed in terms of 56 different categories of how sick you are and then your outcomes are reported relative to those admission characteristics. In the same way the Conservative government has never much liked the idea of value-added; they like contextualised value-added even less. Michael Gove famously said that to use contextualised value-added was to actually expect less from kids from disadvantaged backgrounds. Well, that might happen, but it's like saying that having risk-adjusted mortality stats in the NHS means that doctors won't try hard to save the sickest patients, which is a bizarre claim. The problem is that whenever an assessment is used for one purpose, it weakens its ability to serve another purpose. This is called 'Goodhart's law' in the UK. It's called 'Campbell's law' in the United States.

Originally we started using GCSEs to certify student achievement, but then we started using them to certify school quality, which is bizarre because in England only about 8% of the variation in GCSE scores is caused by the quality of teaching the students receive. The other 92% is actually outside the school's control. So what then happened is we started actually making sure that students were well prepared for these exams. In English literature, for example, we started focusing only on the set book, and then only on the aspects of the set book that are most likely to come up in the tests. There used to be relatively little spoon-feeding at A-level because we saw A-level as a preparation for university study. But if you're under pressure to improve your A-level results, you will make sure your students do well by taking more and more responsibility for their learning away from them. This is the real problem; it's that any assessment changes its characteristics when it's used. You might think that's not a big issue in your school but it is. So if you hold teachers accountable for students' results, you will change how teachers teach. It might be in a good way, it might be in a bad way, but it will distort the system. This is the essence of Campbell's law or Goodhart's law. Any policy indicator loses its usefulness when used as an object of policy – any performance indicator.

Just to wrap up one more point there then: formative and summative aren't descriptions of assessments. There is no such *a* formative or *a* summative assessment because the same assessment can be used formatively or summatively. Let me give an example. I am in a primary school. I'm deciding I want to test this boy's knowledge of his number facts all the way from 1 × 1 up to 10 × 10. I choose 20 of them at random. I quiz him. He gets ten out of 20 right. I can conclude from that that he knows approximately 50% of his number facts. That is a summative conclusion; that's a conclusion about his status. If I notice he's having a particular difficulty with the seven times table, that gives me something to go on; that's a formative conclusion. So the same assessment – and even the same assessment evidence – can be used formatively and summatively.

To draw all that together: validity is a property of conclusions, and formative and summative are properties of conclusions. In other words, we can draw formative conclusions – this child needs help with the seven times table – or summative conclusions – this child knows 50% of his number facts. That I think is really important.

Then we come onto reliability. People talk about validity and reliability. That is in my view unhelpful because you can't have a valid assessment and valid conclusion if the results are unreliable. If the student gets a different score tomorrow from today, if they get a different score if teacher A marks the work rather than teacher B, then any conclusions we draw on the basis of those outcomes will be flawed. So reliability is *part of* validity. Reliability is basically an aspect of scores depending on things they shouldn't. In other words you're asking, 'Was the student lucky in who marked his test?' That's something that affects the score and it shouldn't, so there's an example of scores depending on things they shouldn't. When we come onto the design of whole-school assessment systems, I think it's really important that we don't actually think of there being a perfect assessment system. There isn't and, in fact, assessment systems involve trade-offs. So there is a trade-off with reliability and other aspects of validity.

So if I want a highly reliable result, I would ask a lot of questions on a very narrow topic. If I ask 100 questions on arithmetic, for example, then it's highly unlikely the child will be lucky in the 100 questions I happen to choose. If I ask five questions then they *might* get lucky five times. They're not going to get lucky 100 times. So a very narrow test can have a very high degree of reliability, but your ability to conclude anything about anything else that you didn't test is compromised. The way I like to think about this is in terms of stage lighting. For a given amount of wattage or candle power, you can focus a spotlight and get a lot of information about one part of the stage, or you can use a floodlight and get a little bit of information about everywhere but there's a trade-off. Here's the really important part: if you focus the spotlight on one part of the stage, you have no idea what the actors are getting up to in the areas that are not in the floodlight. This is what we see in high-stakes tests. We actually say, 'This is just a sample, but if the sample is predictable, teachers spend all their time preparing kids for the things that you are counting.' That happens at GCSE now, but it also may happen if you have an assessment system where you hold teachers accountable for getting particular results. So there's always going to be a trade-off here.

So what I like to offer you by way of a conclusion before we go into the Q&A – because I would be interested in hearing what you want to know most about – I think there are five principles that we can think about in the design of an assessment system, although you will never get a system that does all five.

So the first is the assessment is *distributed*. In other words, we're not going to collect the information at the end. We're not going to do a high-stakes exam like they have in the baccalaureate in France or the Abitur in Germany or the A-level in the England. What we're going to do is we're going to collect information over time, which makes our results more reliable. But the assessment system also has to be *synoptic*, because we don't want to end up with the American system, where students do three or four weeks' work on a particular topic, then they get an assessment on that topic and a grade. They then get to bank the grade and they keep that A (if that's what they got), even if they forget everything they needed to know to get the A. So there's a trade-off there between distributed and synoptic. I think we need to collect the information throughout the course of the term or the marking period or the half-term, but we also need students to actually assemble all the things that they've learned together. We need to get away from this idea that students are going to learn stuff and forget it.

The third requirement is that the assessment system is *extensive*. If we only assess reading and writing, then it won't be surprising if teachers don't pay much attention to speaking and listening. We need to be assessing all the things we think are important. Now we won't be able to do some of that as reliably, but I don't think we should make reliability our prime concern. This is a point that's actually worth stating more broadly. I often point out to people that GCSEs are not particularly reliable and that on a given day the average error is at least one grade either way and that I think is a really important point. Any grade has error. Any measurement, in education or otherwise, has error. So, I would like to see teachers reporting scores to students, to parents like this: 'The pass mark for this course is 70 and your child scored 65, so they failed, maybe, but because it's 65 plus or minus 10 (there's error there) your child might have passed. Probably didn't, but 65 plus or minus 10.' To which the parent might say, 'Why don't you know exactly?' 'Every assessment has error.' 'Couldn't you make the assessments more reliable?' 'I could, by taking more time for testing, but that would take time away from teaching and we don't want to do that.'

So, I think we have to regard the inaccuracy – the unreliability – of our assessments as optimal. We don't want more reliable assessments because we'd take far too much testing time to achieve it. What we do therefore need to do is not to place too much weight on an individual result.

Next, the assessment needs to be *extensive*. It needs to be *manageable* so the teacher is going to administer this system without too much extra work, and it needs to be *trusted* by the key stakeholders including parents. So these five principles – distributed, synoptic, extensive, trusted and manageable – are always in tension, but I think they are important principles to bear in mind. There is no perfect assessment system. It involves trade-offs and the trade-off might be explicit and planned, which I think is good, or you can forget about these trade-offs and think you're actually designing a perfect assessment system, in which case there will be trade-offs but you won't know where they are. What I'm suggesting is rather than ending up somewhere where we don't know how we ended up where we are, we need to be designing assessment systems where we are aware of the trade-offs we made in getting that assessment system. We say, 'Yes, that is a trade-off. We decided that this aspect was more important than that aspect and therefore we're able to speak with less authority than we would like on this area, because it's not worth spending more time getting more accurate information.'

So those five principles I think are a helpful starting point and the other thing to remember is that assessments – as well as having meanings – have consequences. So whatever the consequences are, we'll have to factor in, particularly in high school, that students will play the system. They're very smart and they'll find ways of getting the highest score for the least effort and you should design your assessment system to take that into account.

So I think that's probably enough from me on the principles of assessment and now I would like to hand back to John to see if there have been any questions or if anybody wants to ask the questions verbally.

Questions

JT: Where, if anywhere, have you seen the closest to the most ideal assessment system? Have you come across schools that have got it as right as possible?

DW: No. Well, I should say they've got it right for *them*. So, for example, the kind of assessment systems that work in Sweden, work okay if there's very high trust in teachers, but those systems will be a disaster in England, where the government actually cultivates distrust of teachers. Without government interference I think teachers would be trusted far more than they are, but governments consistently undermine public trust in teachers. Therefore, the things that work in Sweden or Finland would not work here because of government's undermining of teacher authority. In some cases that trust needed to be undermined. If the teacher says, 'This is worth a C because I say it's worth a C', well, they deserve everything that happens to them because they should have externalised the standards. This is quite an important point. If we have teacher marking and the teacher doesn't make the criteria for a particular grade as transparent as possible – not necessarily fully transparent – then the grade looks like the teacher's verdict. Students say, 'She gave me a C.' While if the teacher is clear about why that work is only worth a C then the student will say, 'I got a C', but more importantly it repositions the teacher. If the teacher has these subjective, unrevealed standards, then the student sees the teacher as an enemy who judges you. If, on the other hand, the standards are externalised then the teacher is the student's ally against the standard. The teacher is like the high-jump coach who is trying to get the athlete to clear the bar at six feet. I have never heard an athlete who kicks the bar up with their foot as they go over saying, 'Well, that's just your opinion.' We didn't clear the bar. So teachers need to work to make sure as far as they can through exemplification, through description, through rubrics to say, 'This is not worth a B because you didn't actually reach the standard needed for a B in terms of these following aspects.'

JT: That brings me round to how difficult it is to nail down rubrics and criteria. I've listened a lot to Daisy Christodoulou and her comparative judgement process, and I wonder what you thought of going down a comparative judgement route.

DW: Well, the one thing that I haven't stuck my head above the parapet to proclaim from the rooftops is, to mix the metaphor somewhat, *No more marking* is entirely summative. There's no formative benefit in *No more marking*. It just tells you: 'You got a B or a C or a D.' Now that may free teachers to do some formative assessment, but the interesting thing is if we do formative assessment well, our students will know whether their work is worth a B or a C. What they won't know is how to make that C into a B, and that's where the teacher's expertise come in. If we do assessment well, our students will understand the standards. They will be able to say, 'I am here and I need to be here', but the teacher also needs to possess – as well as a sense of quality – an anatomy of quality. What's this next small step that this pupil needs to take to get from where they are to where they need to be? If you look at sports coaching, you will see excellent examples of sports coaches being able to see what's wrong.

So in cricket, for example, there's an orthodoxy that cricket is a side-on game and it kind of is, but it kind of isn't. So you've had many bowlers, a bit like Mike Procter who played for Gloucestershire and South Africa, who had a square on – a very strange – action and bowled off the 'wrong' foot. Everything wrong, but his hips and his shoulders were aligned at the moment of delivery.

So if you see a cricketer with a mixed action, where their shoulders and their hips are not aligned at the moment of delivery, that gives the coach something to work with the athlete on. We see that kind of example all the time in sports, but often we don't see it on the academic side. A great marking activity, for example, I would say is get some teachers to get together, bring some student work, sit down in pairs and take 20 minutes. What will be the best advice you could give to this student now? Just take what normally takes 20 seconds, 30 seconds, and unpack that. What would we say to this child right now to move their learning forward?

Heather De Silva (HDS): Thank you, Dylan. Thinking about what you've said, I feel Covid was a huge benefit. It made teachers have to be collaborative, to work hard to establish the evidence for specific grades.

DW: Well, you're absolutely right about the importance of the evidence, but here's the crucial thing for me. Formative and summative are descriptions of conclusions, not of evidence. What I saw wrong with coursework assessment was that it was first of all entirely summative and secondly, coursework in GCSE was never really coursework. It was not the work of the course. It was an additional requirement tagged on to actually produce some information about things that were not easily assessed through a timed written examination. Then we had problems of authentication, who was doing the work and all that stuff, so we had controlled conditions, which never really worked particularly well, and took time away from teaching. So here's my touchstone. I would like teachers collecting evidence about what is useful to them about their students' progress and keeping that in a mark book of some kind. Then periodically that evidence should be reinterpreted for a summative purpose. So the question is: do teachers use their mark books to plan teaching?

In my view, in most schools, certainly in secondary schools, teachers don't. Mark books are useful for writing school reports and I think we need to think about teachers collecting systematic evidence that is useful to them for the purposes of planning teaching for that group and periodically summarising that in a way that could be reported that I think would be the best way forward. So you have the same evidence being used formatively and summatively. Basically, if you collected evidence for a formative purpose, you can always summarise it to serve a summative purpose. If you collected evidence primarily for a summative purpose, it's often quite difficult to use it for a formative purpose because you haven't got the right evidence in place. So that would be my touchstone for the way that a school is doing this intelligently: are teachers referring to their mark books in planning teaching?

JT: Dylan, can I just come in there? We're going to have to tie this up. This is just a fascinating conversation. A final comment from the chat, 'Surely by this measure summative assessment is not necessary in the majority of primary years as, if the formative assessment is consistent and true and accurate, the children will make the progress they need to make. While we're busy doing pointless summative assessments we are wasting valuable teaching time', which chimes a little bit with what you were saying.

DW: It does but I think that we also can fool ourselves as teachers. So I think there is a space for something like this when you have more than one class in a year group. The idea that the Year 3 teachers get together and plan a test for Year 3. John, if you set a test and your kids get 85 and I set a test and my kids get 75, I don't think I have anything to learn from you because you're a softie and basically you're giving them an easy test standard. On the other hand, if you and I sit down together and decide what our Year 3 children should be able to do by the end of the year, then now if you get 85 and I get 75 as an average, I've run out of excuses. I'm ready to ask you why do your students do so well in that test? So I think having teachers collaboratively plan formal set-piece assessments so that we don't fool ourselves that everything's okay. We do then have that formal jolt to the system, and I think that's really important. So that is a summative assessment, but it's entirely for the purpose of those teachers. It is not for senior management. Senior management should be asking: did the test take place and did we do anything useful with the information? It shouldn't go beyond that and that is the kind of consequence that is helpful.

You see, as soon as senior management start saying, 'I want to see those test results', then teachers will start preparing kids for the tests. The ability of a teacher to give us accurate information about where kids really are diminishes because now the coaching has actually made sure that all the kids do well; it's about trade-offs again.

JT: Yes, and I would be really interested in the sawtooth effect that we do when we get really good at getting children to jump through the hoops that we set them, and that's why we reset all the specs, etc. I make people laugh at the moment when I talk at conferences when I say, 'Look, we really need to confess that we've always made Key Stage 3 data up.' Everybody starts giggling, but largely because it's true, because it's for the wrong audience. It's for heads and accountability.

DW: Especially when they had that ratchet and kids weren't allowed to go down, when in fact all the research we've got suggests that kids often go down. In the Leverhulme Numeracy Research project in primary schools, we found that 90% of kids had a major regression in maths achievement at least once in primary school. They were actually behind six months later where they had been six months earlier, 90% of kids (it was actually 89, 11% of kids were 'normal' in making steady progress).

JT: Flight paths, we've all known flight paths, but yes, they were complete nonsense and I remember slamming my fist on a table at a local authority meeting many moons ago, when we weren't allowed to set headline targets lower than the previous year. I just said, 'When did we start living in a Stalinist state?'

DW: My wife was a headteacher for 20 years and she actually said to the local authority, 'You can put in whatever numbers you like. We don't care. We're just going to work as hard as we can to get the best results for our kids and you can put whatever fictions you like in your planning documents. It's not going to have any impact on what we're doing.'

JT: Dylan, that's a great place to end. Thank you so much. It's been a privilege and a pleasure to have you on our first ever Leadership 55 webinar, really appreciate it. Take good care.

DW: Good fun, thank you.

Chapter 3
Leadership 55 wisdom – the essence of the headteacher's job

The headteacher's job…

What is the essence of a headteacher's job? I would argue that it is ensuring that teachers can *get on* with teaching in a way that provides the best learning experience possible for their pupils. That requires an obsessive focus upon removing every single barrier that's preventing teachers from doing their job.

Indeed, teachers are a headteacher's greatest resource. At Huntington School, where I was headteacher for 14 years, we taught something like 1996 lessons a week; I taught three of them. I was only going to keep my job if the other 1993 lessons were taught well.

The trouble is that the reality of teaching a class of 30 students in a one-hour chunk and getting all of them to make progress in their learning is a complex task beyond comprehension.

Think about it. Unless you have a class of 15 sets of twins, each student in front of you in period 1 on a Tuesday has had different: experiences since they left school on Monday afternoon; amounts of sleep; breakfasts; conversations with parents/carers/friends/relatives/form tutors; recollections of what you taught them last lesson; thoughts about the work in front of them we will never know about; hormones released by their brain; learning experiences since they were born; genome patterns shaping their physiology… You get my meaning.

How on earth can we expect to know that every single student in that one class of 30 students has made the expected progress at the end of one hour of teaching? But too many school leaders want to implement a simple, single, catch-all solution to all teaching and learning ills, as though the teachers' raw materials are wood and steel, not flesh and blood.

Headteachers cannot reduce the complexity of the teaching and learning process. What they *can* do is to make it as simple as possible for their teachers to do the complex job of teaching. Les Walton's view of running schools resonates loudly with my philosophy:

> *You start with the assumption that children are born to learn, teachers want to teach, people want to do a good job and what is stopping them is the system. Your job as a headteacher then is not to motivate or even to encourage them but actually to ask 'what is stopping you doing a good job and how can I remove that barrier?'*[1]

So the best thing a headteacher can do is to find out what is getting in the way of their teachers doing their core job, by seeing what's happening in classrooms and through talking openly to teachers. And then headteachers need to remove every single identified barrier that prevents teachers from teaching. That ranges from ensuring that disruptive pupils disrupt no longer to having a back-up to the computer system so that connectivity is 100% guaranteed. It's that simple…

---

1   Roberts, J. (2020) 'Teachers want to teach, the system is stopping them', *TES Magazine*. www.tes.com/magazine/archive/teachers-want-teach-system-stopping-them.

Chapter 4
A conversation on SEND with Margaret Mulholland

This is a great opportunity to talk to you about leading special educational needs. Before we start, I want to highlight four areas that we might think about today as school leaders. I want to think about who we are talking about when we talk about SEND. Then about who's on the SEND team in your school. I'd like you to start thinking about that now. I thought we should also touch on Ofsted and why, in the context of SEND, there are some quite positive things happening. We'll reflect on that. And then to finish with the zeitgeist of the moment: adaptive teaching. Everybody's doing adaptive teaching, and I'm delighted about that. But I think we need to really think about why we need some core principles around that, enabling us to do assessment and not assumption in driving adaptive teaching.

Let's begin with the leadership of SEND. I feel like a bit of a one-trick pony on this, but the reason that I'm sharing the same key messages across the country at the moment is because I've been very lucky over the last few years to work on a number of large projects, firstly for the Education Endowment Foundation, looking at the impact of the SEND review. Loads of schools will have used that document. It's a white-label document, and lots of people use it to self-evaluate. The EEF have looked at it as one of their best bets in relation to supporting leadership of SEND. Katherine Walsh, who has also worked in Haringey, and I did an 18-month programme working with 160 schools, 72 intervention schools, predominantly secondary, looking at how that SEND review tool can be utilised. I think there are some really key things that add value: it's not about the SENDCO sitting in an office doing a self-evaluation; it's about a whole-school approach. One of the things that we learned in the course of leading that programme with those schools was that the key thing was that they took the lead and developed autonomy. Having a consultant or a parent do that review can be helpful, but the ownership has to be with the school. We've then gone on to do a similar programme with 60 schools in York, which has been really interesting working with the Pathfinder Teaching School Hub. They developed a SEND champions programme. This programme took interested staff from across the school. In some schools, like Huntington School, for example, it was a science teacher who wanted to be the SEND champion and lead the programme of change across the school. So it was really about taking the school's own drivers and enhancing and supporting them.

I think it's fair to say that all schools are on a rapid and positive journey from SEND being 'othered' in the way the systems and processes historically have shaped the way we provide for SEND and look after young people with special educational needs. We've often looked at special educational needs as siloed, segregated and separated. All the research from Rob Webster's SEND studies reflects this systemic behaviour. But schools are really on a rapid journey of moving from that othered, siloed view of SEND to establishing a much more integrated and built-in model of SEND. I think that journey is what we want to look at today. What are those four areas of that journey? Moving from an operational model of SEND, where we talk about SEND as though it's something separate, with some of the pedagogy relating to it, to a strategic model of leadership for SEND in our settings. That means, as this diagram shows, thinking about SEND centrally and intrinsically for school improvement, culture and pedagogy.

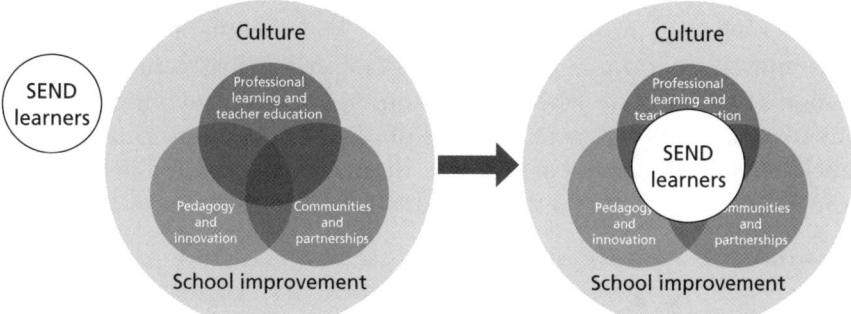

So then the question is: how do we establish systems and processes that enable that to happen? My provocation to you is: if we do adaptive teaching to change the pedagogy to be more inclusive, and we're not changing our systems and processes – the way we lead and embed SEND across the school system – then all the good work we're trying to establish in the classroom will not have the desired impact. That means we really need to think about what it looks like in practice.

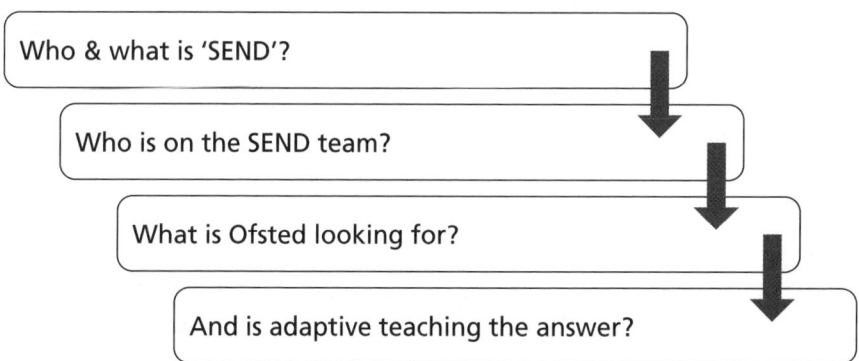

So we're going to look at these four reflections. Who and what is SEND? In other words, what do we mean by SEND in our school? Are we all on the same page? Who's on the SEND team? And as we move forward through school improvement, what is Ofsted looking for, and is adaptive teaching the answer?

Who is SEND?

Who is SEND? When we ask this question, we often think about the children who are on the SEND register. I know many of you here will have moved on from this, and I'm establishing this picture more to recognise and capture where you're coming from and moving towards, but we default too often to a model of SEND in relation to diagnostic labels, a medical model. For example, there are four children in this class who are autistic; there are three children who are dyslexic.

This medical model of SEND still has some traction in schools today and we need to move away from it quickly. It's not that labels aren't helpful, but they can deskill teachers and potentially leaders as well. Many leaders, when I ask about children with SEND, will defer to their SENDCO. That is not just about deferment; it's about confidence and expertise. So that notion of expertise around SEND is something that the research questions, and something that we should be questioning too.

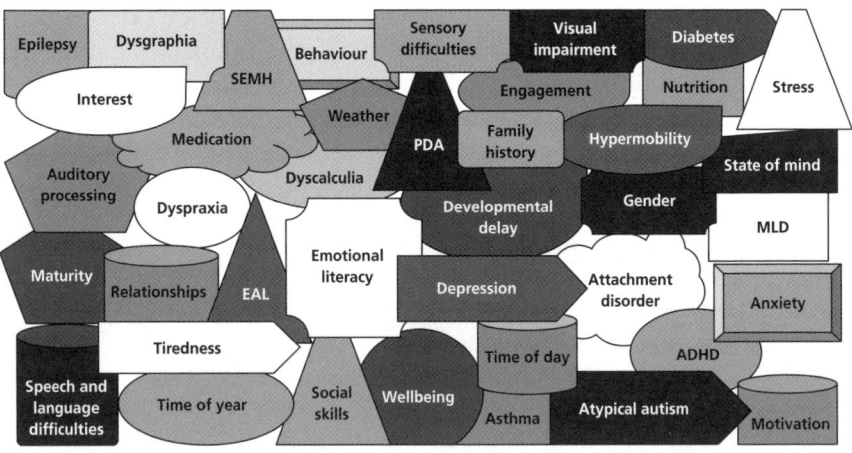

This hugely complex slide was drawn up by Mandy K., an early career teacher at the time. It is a really good example of the historic view of what a classroom can look like when we talk about SEND as a diagnostic label. If this is the notion of SEND and the expertise we require for the classroom, then we deskill our teachers. How can one be an expert in all of that?

I'm not an expert in all that, but I know that on a Tuesday morning, it might be the fact that a child is tired or hungry that's going to influence their behaviours and learning, rather than the fact that they're dyslexic or dyspraxic. These labels can be helpful signposts, but, in a sense, they overwhelm and deskill. We don't need to be experts in everything there and we need to make sure that message gets across in schools. This medical signposting is a starting point, something that a SENDCO or even Google can help us with, but what we are already experts in is knowing our pupils.

When we look at the expertise required for SEND, the skill sets and genuinely deep knowledge we need are around understanding the learner. The systems and processes that service our knowledge of each child tell us about their labels but also help us establish a deeper understanding of what that child can and can't do, which is really important. Marc Rowland often uses the phrase 'Assessment, not assumption'. We make assumptions about what a child can do, which is where the label of SEND can get in the way of understanding a child's capabilities. If we see them as a child with SEND in a maths lesson and make judgements about their ability to remember or apply times tables, but then the next day see that they have good visual or spatial awareness for shapes, are we limiting our expectations? In relation to (Core Teacher Standards) Standard One being 'holding high expectations of learners', are we reducing expectations if we don't use assessment rather than assumption? I think that's a key message around who we are talking about: we're talking about pupils, not labels. We're talking about individuals with distinct profiles.

And that's not to mention that these labels are almost redundant now because very few children experience just one barrier to learning. A young person with learning difficulties can often experience co-occurring needs, so we need a more flexible notion of expertise to move beyond those labels.

As school leaders, we must have confidence in the population we're considering when thinking about strategies and action planning. The national figure for children in school with SEND is now 17.3%, up from 16.6% the previous year. EHCP numbers have already surpassed the half-million mark, but it's still a minority. It's a significant minority, but I think the perception of it being a minority is problematic. When thinking about strategy, curriculum accessibility or adaptations, is it helpful to think about percentage or should we think more broadly and agilely? That's a national perspective, but it's worth asking: do all your staff in your school know your stats? It doesn't matter if they're much higher or lower, but is everybody aware? It's really important that everybody is aware of the profile of need in your school.

Previously, I was visiting schools in Uxbridge and discussing the profile of need. Interestingly, only *some* people in the leadership team were aware of the profile in their school. If their dominant need is speech, language and communication, the next question should automatically be: how does your curriculum reflect those needs? But if the history lead, for example, doesn't know that speech, language and communication is the dominant need, then they won't address oracy in the same way. They're not looking at why the whole-school approach is so relevant, pertinent and reflective of the broader spectrum of needs within the school. So, it is important to ask: what are our dominant needs? Does everybody know, and how does our curriculum respond to that?

When we think about our classrooms, we realise there's far more than just a handful of young people who find learning difficult. The Education Policy Institute[2] tracked cohorts from reception through to Year 11 for three years, and they determined that the percentage of young people who had ever been on the SEND register was around 40%, and in one year, it was 44%. We know many young people who go on to have learning difficulties identified beyond school and were never on the SEND register. Are we, then, talking about a minority or are we talking about a significant proportion of young people who find learning difficult?

I think the evidence suggests that we shouldn't frame our response or strategy around that 17.3%. We should consider what our curriculum looks like for that 40%. How are those adaptations serving a broader picture of difficulty, even difficulty that might be temporary? Should we not be responsive, rather than having a narrowing perspective?

---

2   Education Policy Institute and Hutchinson, J. (2017) How many children have SEND? https://essexprimaryheads.co.uk/files/how-many-children-are-identified-with-send-education-policy-institute-nov-2017.pdf.

Ofsted and SEND

We know everybody in the school wants to be inclusive; I've never met a teacher who doesn't want to be inclusive. What are the barriers that exist to adopting holistic and inclusive strategies? In the past, we used to say Ofsted was the barrier, but we can't say that anymore. In terms of inclusion and ensuring the curriculum is meeting everybody's needs, particularly those with SEND, Ofsted has been clear in the new framework. They are now looking at how the curriculum adapts for those young people. Your overall effectiveness would be and is impacted if your staff in each classroom aren't familiar with who has SEND or who finds learning difficult. If they can't address that, then that's an issue.

> Inspectors will evaluate evidence of the impact of the curriculum, including on the most disadvantaged pupils. This includes pupils with SEND.

> Inspectors will take a rounded view of the quality of education that a school provides to all its pupils, including the most disadvantaged pupils and pupils with SEND.

> Quality of education – 'good' the curriculum is successfully adapted, designed or developed to be ambitious and meet the needs of pupils with SEND, developing their knowledge, skills and abilities to apply what they know and can do with increasing fluency and independence.

> Before making the final judgement on overall effectiveness, inspectors will always consider the spiritual, moral, social and cultural development of pupils at the school, and evaluate the extent to which the school's education provision meets different pupil's needs, including pupils with SEND.

Go back to the picture from before about the medical model of SEND deskilling teachers and staff dealing with SEND, and align that picture with these Ofsted expectations. Our teachers do know the young people and what they need. They know their strengths and how to build on them. But sometimes they don't recognise that those adaptive strategies are what Ofsted is looking for. When their perceptions of meeting the needs of children with SEND are tied to labels, it can hinder them from articulating how they've adapted seating, scaffolds, activities or starter tasks to meet the needs of different classes. Those are the things that Ofsted is looking for, along with a robust rationale. If we're clear about knowing the learner as a fundamental aspect, I think it empowers our teachers.

Chris Pollitt, an HMI who hosts helpful Ofsted webinars, asks a particularly brilliant question: does your curriculum remove barriers to learning, or does it create barriers to learning? Middle leaders can reflect on this question repeatedly when considering their curriculum and its accessibility for all pupils. There's also the question of who reviews SEND at a school? The SENDCO or everyone? The clue is in the question, isn't it?

Who is on the SEND team?

That leads us nicely on to who is on your SEND team. Traditionally, we had a very operational model of SEND. When asked who was on the SEND team, headteachers would always say, 'The SENDCO and the TAs'. Recently, someone beautifully said to me at a conference, 'Margaret, I'm here with my SENDCO. I'm a headteacher, and she and I know that my SEND team includes our middle leaders – everyone is responsible for SEND.' Those middle leaders are driving SEND in a distributed leadership model. The headteacher and the SENDCO knew that, because they were the ones establishing that change. However, they were concerned that not everyone in their school had fully embraced the concept of distributed leadership and the shift from the SENDCO leading the team to school leaders and the leadership team strategically driving SEND as a central tenet of school development.

I'm going to stop on this for a moment because it's so fundamental. When I think about the phrase 'everyone is a teacher of SEND' or 'every leader is a leader of SEND', I think one of the problems we identified during the EEF trial was that schools thought being strategic meant sharing the SENDCO's workload, giving them more time and sharing responsibilities and accountabilities. But we missed a crucial point: it wasn't the shared responsibility and accountability that needed to be the focus; it was shared knowledge. The SENDCO, stuck on the hamster wheel of workload, had all the knowledge of the learners with SEND and was trying to distribute it to the rest of the school.

We had an example where a SENDCO spent – not untypically – 25 days in one-to-one meetings with parents and IEP meetings. That's not very strategic. The problem wasn't her time but the knowledge she had acquired and how it was disseminated and shared. When a child was dysregulated in the classroom, who had the knowledge to support that de-escalation of behaviour or to navigate a change in pedagogy? Only the SENDCO. Even if people had read the one-page profile, they didn't have the vested interest. So how do we ensure that shared responsibility includes shared knowledge? That was an interesting finding we hadn't really considered.

Who plans and delivers maths interventions?

```
SENDCO → TAs → Maths HoD → Maths teachers

Maths teachers ← Maths HoD ↔ SENDCO
              ↓
             TAs
```

This is an example of a school thinking hard about how to disseminate the knowledge of the child, that key element we were talking about as the skill and knowledge required by all teachers. They used the example of interventions and found that in many instances, both primary and secondary, the SENDCO was determining the literacy and numeracy interventions, but that was not being effectively disseminated to the class teachers. This is a secondary model, but the primary schools told us the same thing.

Despite all the guidance we have from the EEF in terms of what makes a good intervention, that 'build back better' – to use a government phrase – was not happening very well because the teachers didn't have the knowledge of the intervention. That became a barrier in terms of understanding the learners; the separation between the SENDCO and the maths department was too great for real engagement. A child would attend a pull-out intervention and return to class without being enabled to move forward and make progress.

In this example, the secondary school had to rethink their model, realising that distributed leadership must include distributed knowledge. It had to start with the head of department and SENDCO determining the intervention together, outlining its core elements, and then sharing that information with teachers to build on the support staff's work more effectively.

This example highlights distributed leadership systems and processes that can enable adaptive practice to make sense. You can't adapt teaching if you don't have the knowledge of the specific learner and intervention in order to build. We have brilliant work happening around adaptive pedagogy, but without the systems and processes to support shared adaptive knowledge, it can't reach all parts of schooling.

Adaptive teaching

That brings us to adaptive teaching. We have a dilemma and a misconception brewing around differentiation and adaptive teaching. I'm a big fan of adaptive teaching and always have been, but I find myself defending differentiation a little bit because there's a misconception that differentiation itself is a problem. Poorly implemented differentiation can be an issue, but it is supportive of young people who need specialist support, especially in mainstream settings. There is a place for differentiation, but the driver for adaptive teaching is that it is absolutely crucial for universal provision.

Adaptive teaching enables staff to respond to needs without resorting to bad practices, like creating a separate lesson for every child in the class. Shared outcomes, and how we achieve them, are essential.

Regarding adaptive teaching, I always use the analogy of a detective. Great detectives are great teachers, and vice versa. When a child gets stuck in their learning, what do we do? In a special setting, they wouldn't rely on the label and say, 'What do we do when an autistic child gets stuck?' They would look closely at what's happening for this child and find what's driving that next step. A SENDCO would refer to the graduated approach: assess, plan, do, review. But I, with my mainstream hat on, would say it's formative assessment. Formative assessment is what drives the next step. It's what you learn from the child.

Someone mentioned to me recently that they worry their class is only composed of task-oriented pedagogy. If teachers are just moving from task to task without developing those tasks to learn more about the children in front of them, we're missing the point. We are the learners in that instance if we're going to improve adaptive planning. This is a big issue. We should be practising those 'noticing' skills and embedding them in the classroom. We're used to a 'learn that' and 'learn how to…' model; the 'learn why' that threads everything together is what gives autonomy to the adaptive expert in the classroom. We need to focus on assessment, not assumption, and use strategies based on that.

How do we embed those strategies? I was talking to someone in Hull recently who was doing an INSET forum, and he mentioned that they developed pedagogy circles that ran for 15–20 minutes once a week, where they focus on reflective pedagogy to develop adaptive skills. Where does that exist in our systems and processes? It shouldn't be added in or bolted on. Is it in departmental meetings? Is it in mentoring for ECF? Where can we ensure that this knowledge of the child is being developed and stretched as part of the systems and processes we already have in place?

I go back to the evidence base around this. It might sound like I'm talking a lot about skills and dispositions – and I am – but the evidence around cognitive science supports that. One of my favourite people in the education world, Linda Darling-Hammond, a Californian researcher and system leader, says that we're on the right track with this. However, we cannot develop adaptive teaching without developing adaptive expertise.

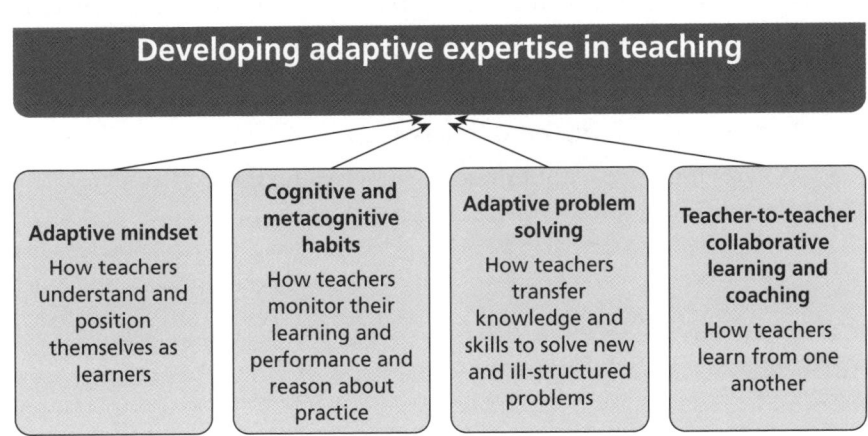

These are the component parts of adaptive expertise. I think we've got some of this right: focusing on cognitive and metacognitive habits and developing an adaptive mindset. But we need to build systems and processes that promote adaptive problem solving and teacher-to-teacher collaboration. Without these elements, adaptive teaching won't improve; it will just become a one-size-fits-all approach, which is not its purpose.

It's interesting to dwell on what we mean by 'adaptive expertise'. This concept comes from research that highlights its importance from the beginning of a teacher's career, not something developed years into the profession. By then, we might have deskilled our teachers. This is about learning to be agile and teaching the child right from day one, teaching nuance, not just routines. Routines are crucial, but we must also focus on adaptability from the start. There is fascinating research around this from the Ministry of Defence. They've done significant work on how adaptive expertise develops, because in combat, if you don't adapt from day one, you're dead.

Tying it all together

And finally, how does this all fit together? I think this framework that looks at what all educators need to know and be able to do is a lovely reflective tool again from the research of Linda Darling-Hammond and her colleagues at the Learning Policy Institute. It is not SEND-specific but pedagogic and inclusive of all learners. It helps us think about:

- Where are we strong at the moment?
- Where are we doing good things as a school that we can build on?
- Where might we want to nudge ourselves further?

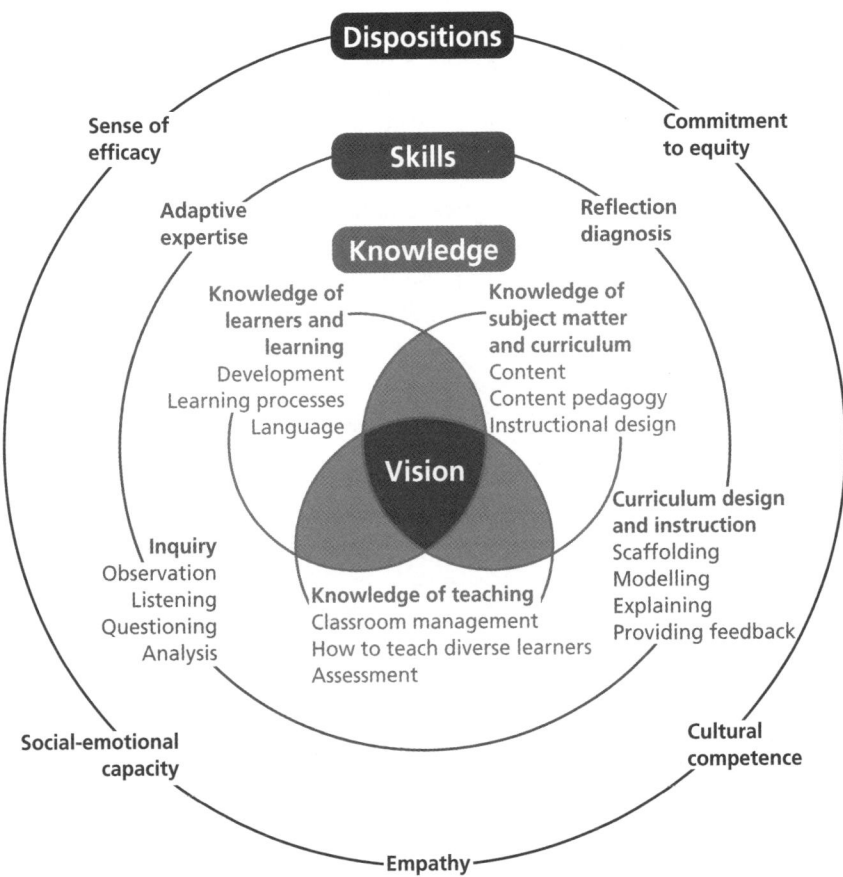

Source: Darling-Hammond, L., Flook, L., Schachner, A. and Wojcikiewicz, S. (with Cantor, P. and Osher, D.) (2021) 'Educator learning to enact the science of learning and development', Learning Policy Institute. Available at: https://doi.org/10.54300/859.776

We're doing a lot of good things in that central zone. Knowledge development *should* be central, but those skills and dispositions to mobilise knowledge are key. We need to give our systems and processes more opportunities to develop that adaptive expertise and inquiry because otherwise, we can't apply that knowledge in the way we need to take care of individuals with learning difficulties.

Language around SEND is key. We're often looking at the problems, not the strengths. But actually if we look at the strengths in the system and in children, there are plenty. Building on the good work we're doing around teaching and learning and a knowledge-based curriculum, we can enhance the offer for all young people if we reframe our thinking about what these things mean for children who find learning hard and put that central to our steps rather than an afterthought.

I was pleased to hear that some schools take sections of the SEND Teacher Handbook and share them across the whole school regularly. What's brilliant about that handbook is that it doesn't specifically mention SEND because it doesn't need to; it's about good inclusive pedagogy and accessible teaching with subject-specific guidance to help think about children who struggle to learn. It's great for subject leaders, both primary and secondary.

And that's my whirlwind tour of SEND.

Questions

John Tomsett (JT): Should there be more than one SEND champion in a school?

Margaret Mulholland (MM): I was a bit sceptical about the SEND Champions programme. I genuinely felt that the key people to mobilise this are the SENDCO and the leadership team. Who do I want to see the SENDCO working with most? The teaching and learning lead in the school – that's who I think is number one on their team. But when you're working with 60 schools on a SEND Champions programme, I was uncertain about the mobilisation of change. Who is the most appropriate agent of change in school? Is the SENDCO, the head, the teaching and learning lead? The truth is: everyone has their role to play. However, it really depends on those players being fully engaged with the commitment to inclusion.

The science teacher from Huntington School, for example, has been amazing. As part of the programme, they've attended events with the SENDCO, participated in online coaching and contributed their own perspectives on what needs to change. It's not about me being an expert; it's about asking the right questions to give them the space to mobilise what they know needs to happen. I think that has really worked. The key for them was to go back and work with their school team and determine who they needed on board to take on that journey.

JT: Hypothetically, a school has a lot of children who have a diagnosis of ADHD. The parents of these children say they are not able to modify their behaviours in any way. If those children are disrupting the classroom, then that's unavoidable. If class teachers try to stop that, then they are discriminating against the children. Do you have any guidance for the class teacher on managing both the parents and the classroom in that example?

MM: That is really difficult for the class teacher. If that was coming up as one of the issues in terms of self-evaluation and action planning, we'd be asking: what's the root of that? I would want to take the next step by working with the parents to consider what executive function issues are present. If we don't address these together now, how will they manage when entering the world of work or an internship?

There's a significant amount of work needed, especially now more than pre-Covid, to rebuild parents' confidence in this area. As a parent of a child with special needs, I understand that parents often don't know what's happening in school. This can lead to critiques from a place of not being part of the journey. Some schools have started to target parent engagement and build champions within the parent community, but I realise it's harder than ever now.

I would also recommend looking at the ADHD Foundation; they are absolutely brilliant. They champion the notion of neurodiversity and celebrate it, promoting a message of enabling rather than just tolerating.

JT: How can we use SEND resources that are accessible for all staff in a school?

MM: The EEF *SEN in Mainstream Schools Guidance Report* and the *Teacher Handbook: SEND* are two key resources. I worked with the EEF to develop the mainstream guidance report, and I think it's really helpful as an enabler to all staff. The way the EEF crafted it is robust and helps teachers to better understand their role. Before we move on to the handbook, the 'SEND Five-a-Day' can be a really helpful resource, too. However, it slips into the danger zone (if not contextualised) of assuming all children start in the same place, which they don't. It's important to recognise where each child is in their development and knowledge, understand their prior learning and build on that.

If I were thinking about the *Teacher Handbook: SEND*, I would start with the subject-specific guidance to hook subject teachers in and let them see how relevant it is for their subject pedagogy. The handbook is hyperlinked, so you can link to your specific subject for primary or secondary and disseminate that across your phase or department team. What I love is that it addresses specific teacher actions, like how to support learners with sensory integration issues or poor working memory. We're not working through labels; we're addressing barriers, which is really helpful.

Chapter 5
Leadership 55 wisdom – establishing your core purpose

I had no idea where the school was heading when I began my first headship. All I could do was replicate some of the behaviours I had learned from observing the several headteachers I had served under. I made some awful mistakes in that first term, nearly all in how I interacted with people. I was quite hapless, in so many ways. And it was all short-termism. I just dealt with the next issue confronting me. As JFK said, 'Effort and courage are not enough without purpose and direction.'

Fortunately, at the end of that first term, Sue Ellis, one of the deputy headteachers, attended a newly developed Investors in People leadership course. She returned insisting that we establish a core purpose for our school. I had completed my NPQH in 2000 and I remembered being told something about Pepsi's core purpose being 'Beat Coke', but beyond that

I was clueless about what a core purpose was and why we might need one. Sue said, pithily, that a core purpose should encapsulate the reason we get up in the morning and come to work.

After some false starts and endless consultations, we came up with the distinctly unpithy core purpose: 'To inspire everyone in our school community with a love of learning and, by doing so, maximise their life chances'. About a year after we had splattered this core purpose around the school and over all our literature, Di Fitzgerald, head of drama, pointed out that it was grammatically incorrect and should have read '...maximise *his or her* life chances'. Despite our illiterate ways, our core purpose really stuck, and three years later it resonated throughout the school, to the point where, according to one of our students, at the beginning of *Romeo and Juliet,* Lord and Lady Capulet wanted Juliet to marry Paris *to maximise her life chances...*

Huntington's core purpose, established as soon as I began my headship there in 2007, was 'To inspire confident learners who will thrive in a changing world'. It stood the test of time. It influenced everything we did.

And every word counts. We all strive, not just to teach, but to *inspire* our learners; building *confidence* is essential for all of us to succeed; we are all *learners,* including the staff; rather than just succeed we would rather *thrive*, which suggests that we are happy both in our career and in our relationships with other people; as technology develops we find ourselves in an ever-*changing world.*

We did have *students* but replaced it with *learners.* Many schools have a line about everyone being a learner, but we really mean it. Learning something helps you understand as a teacher what it is like to be a learner and to struggle at learning something. *Teacher* learning is central to Huntington School's success and every single member of staff had to accept the professional obligation to try to get better at what they do if they worked at Huntington.

We worked hard on getting the wording of our core purpose absolutely right. It was pedantic stuff. The students chose the word *thrive,* where we had used the word *succeed.* I like the word *thrive.* Think about it – plants *thrive* when the conditions for growth are right. And I think the job of headteacher is to get the conditions for growth right in a school. When the conditions for growth are right, students and staff will *thrive*.

So, why is a core purpose so important in your day-to-day running of the school? Well, the process of establishing that core purpose was crucial in helping me understand how to lead a school. When I had to make a tough decision, I returned to the core purpose and considered whether taking that tough decision was aligned with our core purpose. If it was, then that gave me the courage to make the decision, no matter how tough it might have been. And now, 21 years on, that still holds true. Most importantly, however, defining your core purpose allows you to put learning at the heart of everything you do – surely the core business of every school.

Truly great schools will have a core purpose that is timeless and was established way before you begin your headship. That said, there are many schools that are purposeless. Literally. So, if you are appointed to lead a school that has no discernible reason for existing, here are my top five tips for headteachers for *establishing your core purpose*:

1. **Avoid developing your core purpose within the four walls of your office.** You are unlikely to establish an effective core purpose that unites the whole school community if you and your inner-circle SLT impose their core purpose upon the school.

2. **Consult everyone** who might have the remotest interest in your school doing well. It matters that everyone is involved in shaping your core purpose. That process takes weeks, and, while the creative process is messy, it is essential. When developing your core purpose, brief the governors on your intentions and then begin with your staff – *every single one of them*. Your colleagues need to contribute their understanding of why they work at their school if they are going to unite behind the new core purpose. If you get the process of developing a core purpose right, when the caretakers are putting out yet another 250 chairs for the morning's assembly, they'll tell you they're helping the school fulfil its core purpose.

3. **Make your core purpose pithy**, memorable and easy to recite.

4. **Strive to articulate a core purpose that belongs precisely to your school.** I know it is really hard to avoid developing something clichéd. As I demonstrated above, *every word counts*.
5. **Every chance you get to publicise your core purpose, publicise it!** I know it's prosaic, but good signage is worth every penny. And your core purpose should be one of the first things anyone sees when they access your website. That said, better to live your core purpose than to laminate it.

Chapter 6
A conversation on leading writing with Alex Quigley

I want to talk about the leadership of writing. However, the more I think about it, the harder it becomes to separate writing from literacy, or indeed writing from reading. They are two sides of the same coin and they are also deeply connected to talk, home-school planning and continuing professional development (CPD). I believe this broader sense of literacy will come through naturally and we'll likely explore it further in discussion as well.

To begin, I'd like to reflect on the problem. For most people here, it's about holding up a mirror to this challenge. There's a post-Covid challenge to address, alongside a long-standing one related to writing. Post-Covid, we're seeing overt issues reflected in national outcomes. At Key Stage 1, the data clearly shows an impact and we saw it again last year at Key Stage 2. While it may not be as directly visible in secondary outcomes, the reality is that writing underpins and mediates all secondary school results. It must, therefore, be having a collateral impact.

We know the effects on the youngest children are likely to be more pronounced, and this could have repercussions lasting a decade or more. It's not simply a case of saying, 'The pandemic has eased, they're back in the classroom, and we'll pick up where we left off.' There are significant factors here that we need to confront and address.

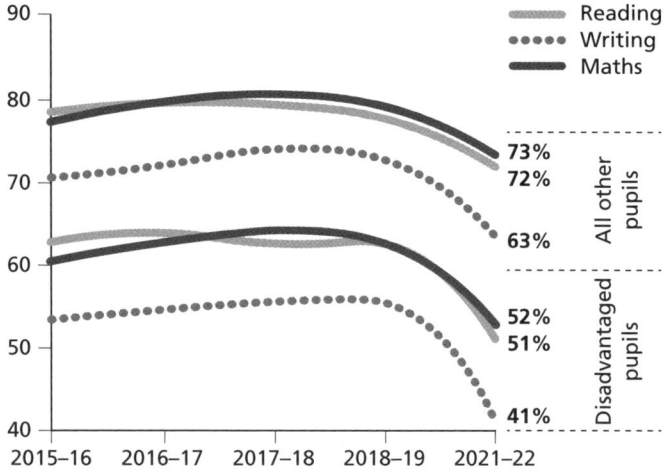

I recently came across data from the Department for Education that struck a chord with me. It highlighted a vital issue, particularly for disadvantaged pupils. We don't fully understand why this is the case, but in writing, we can see that line at the bottom – plummeting. It suggests writing is uniquely sensitive to what happens in the classroom and to the quality of teaching. When pupils miss out on that exposure, whether due to disruptions during the pandemic or other factors, the impact is especially stark for very young children. These children often lack the essential foundations – handwriting, spelling, even basic letter formation.

By the time they reach Years 1 and 2, or even Years 5 and 6, the expectations for their writing haven't changed. However, these pupils haven't had the same level of practice or secured the same foundational skills as their peers. This disparity is becoming increasingly evident.

I speak to many schools and teachers across different phases, key stages and subjects. While the specific problems vary, the underlying challenges are remarkably consistent. Common issues include writing stamina, resilience, the ability to produce extended pieces, editing skills, and motivation. A clear pattern emerges from these conversations.

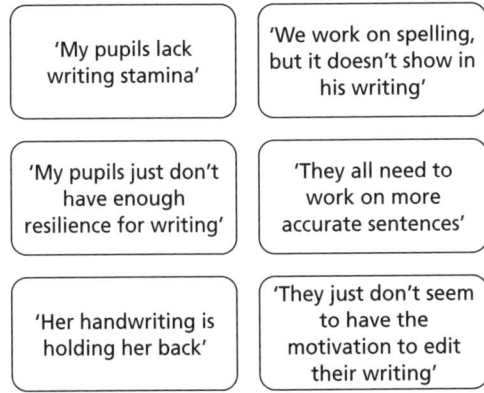

Some challenges are highly visible. For example, in primary schools, spelling is a prominent and obvious indicator of writing struggles, as are punctuation and accuracy. However, other challenges are less visible, such as the background knowledge required for engaging and precise writing, or the vocabulary students need to draw on every time they write.

To address these issues, we need to move beyond broad claims and dig deeper. Improving sentence accuracy, for instance, isn't something a pre-packaged grammar scheme can solve. It requires years of sustained, high-quality, deliberate practice. Accuracy is tied to the quality of ideas; it's not just about constructing a grammatically correct sentence. Addressing this challenge demands teacher expertise, a long-term commitment and consistent, high-quality teaching.

The principles of writing

I want to focus on some key principles. These are informed by a combination of factors: the evidence base around writing development, insights I gained while writing my book, and anecdotal observations from schools and feedback from teachers. Writing has always been a challenging area, but the realities of the post-Covid landscape have made these challenges even more pressing. My hope is that these principles will act as both a mirror for leaders to reflect on their current practices and a window to identify areas where we can concentrate our efforts for maximum impact.

The first principle is that we need to shrink the challenge of writing. Too often, we try to maintain the same standards and practices as before. For example, in Year 5, we aim to cover every genre or, in Year 9, we try to deliver the full curriculum as though nothing has changed. But in doing so, many pupils are falling behind. They're not managing to keep up because they lack the foundational skills to succeed. Instead, we need to focus on the fundamentals of what actually improves writing.

The evidence strongly suggests that crafting great sentences is the best starting point. We should prioritise over-learning and over-practising at the sentence level. This doesn't just improve accuracy – it boosts confidence and enhances style. Mastering sentence-level skills has countless benefits. However, the evidence doesn't advocate for elaborate standardisation processes or formulaic approaches to defining 'good writing', as we often see in Year 6 national assessments. These assessments sometimes lead to over-scaffolded writing or even poor-quality work. Instead, the research points to simplifying the process and homing in on sentence-level precision to build better writing habits.

An analogy I often return to – borrowed from Daisy Christodoulou – is about the need to replace writing marathons with sprints. I remember when Daisy visited Huntington and she discussed assessment in general terms. Her insights resonate deeply with what I've observed, particularly in primary schools but also in secondary settings. Too often, we ask pupils to produce five-paragraph essays, PEE (point, evidence, explanation) paragraphs, or full narrative chapters. These are writing marathons. While pupils are technically writing, they aren't learning much. Instead, they're ingraining poor habits and making repeated errors. Teachers are then left with the difficult task of managing extensive feedback for tasks that have overwhelmed pupils.

By focusing on sentence-level work, we can shrink the task and improve outcomes. This means practising more sprints: short, focused writing tasks that allow pupils to refine specific skills. For example, in secondary schools, my training often focuses on crafting strong, precise sentences in subjects like science, analytical sentences in geography or creative writing in English. Instead of tackling lengthy pieces riddled with errors, we might focus on concise exercises – like crafting a seven-word story – where precision and creativity can flourish. These shorter tasks are more manageable for both pupils and teachers and allow us to give targeted feedback that drives improvement.

As part of advocating for writing less, I am actively suggesting that we should do fewer large writing tasks – fewer 'big writes' and fewer under-scaffolded writing activities. Instead, we need to fill that gap with more reading. Too often, our current model mirrors the expectations of GCSE English language or Year 6 SATs. This leads to a pattern of three-paragraph texts followed by four or five comprehension questions, creating a sort of 'bite-sized, fast-food' approach to reading and writing. It's neither satisfying nor nourishing.

We need to rethink how we can expand opportunities for reading. Through more reading, pupils gain exposure to language, vocabulary and the patterns of good writing. These are vital building blocks that underpin successful writing. To improve writing outcomes, we must increase the volume of reading while reducing the volume of writing. This is a widespread challenge, but I understand some of the systemic drivers working against this approach – expectations for standardisation, pressures to produce data in Year 8 and other requirements that conflict with what the evidence suggests for improving writing.

Another key factor is the need for subject-specific writing, which should begin earlier than we might have traditionally considered. The evidence suggests that this can and should start in primary school. For example, writing like a historian involves choosing specific language to explain significance, describe causes and use the specialised vocabulary of history. Even in Key Stage 1, pupils can begin to develop these skills. In Year 2, while discussing the Great Fire of London, much of the work might occur at the spoken level. However, we should also ask: how can we create great sentences in Year 2?

The seeds we plant in Years 2, 3 and 4 lay the foundation for the writing outcomes we aim for at GCSE. The investment made in these early years prevents a frantic 'last-mile' scramble to fix persistent writing challenges later. By focusing on embedding strong, subject-specific writing skills from an early age, we can reduce the pressures that come with trying to remedy deficiencies further down the line.

Professional development

My final principle focuses on professional development. Teachers are crying out for high-quality, sustained professional development. We know that Ofsted has placed reading and writing high on their agenda, but the question is: what should we do about it? It's not about reacting to a vague whisper of what Ofsted might have mentioned in a local report. Instead, it's about investing in the meaningful, long-term development of teachers' understanding.

What makes good writing? How do you support its development over time? These are complex questions that require thoughtful answers. I taught English for 15 years and there was often an unspoken assumption that I inherently knew how to address all aspects of writing. However, I realised there were significant gaps in my own knowledge. Years later, I feel more confident in this area, but I meet many teachers who lack that same confidence, particularly when it comes to supporting struggling writers.

This challenge has only grown in the wake of Covid, with many children falling behind expected standards. Teachers are under pressure, and time is limited to address these gaps effectively. High-quality professional development must therefore equip teachers with the tools, strategies and understanding to improve writing outcomes – not just for all pupils, but especially for those who need it most.

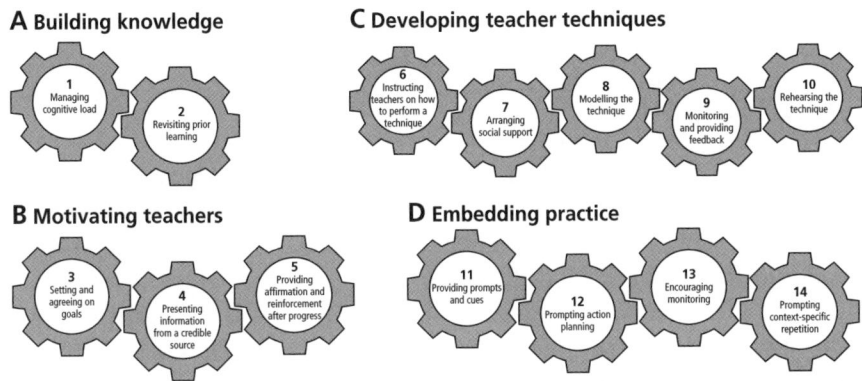

Source: Quigley, A. (2022) *Closing the Writing Gap*. Routledge.

The writing curriculum

Lawrence Stenhouse is my favourite thinker on curriculum and I'd like to borrow – and slightly adapt – one of his ideas:

> *Curriculum development must rest on teacher development, and it should promote it and hence the professionalism of the teacher. Curriculum development translates ideas into classroom practicalities and thereby helps the teacher to strengthen her practice by systematically and thoughtfully testing ideas.*

While we may have a new Ofsted framework, it's worth remembering that teachers and educational professionals have been thinking deeply about curriculum for decades – long before I was even a proverbial twinkle. The alignment between teacher development and curriculum development is essential, and the more I work with schools, speak to leaders and teachers, and observe lessons, the clearer it becomes that literacy development follows the same principles.

In the research, writing is often described as the 'poor sibling' of the three Rs – reading, mathematics and writing. It's under-researched, under-resourced and often overshadowed. Yet the realities of Covid and its impact on outcomes for both younger children and older students are showing us that writing cannot remain the poor sibling. It needs and deserves focused support, quality training and sustained attention. If we address this properly, it could mean less marking, less onerous feedback and fewer hours spent correcting errors. Instead, we could focus on more effective, targeted approaches that have a real impact on the pupils who need them most.

These are the principles I hold, rooted in the best available evidence and what practice is teaching us. Reflecting on the Education Endowment Foundation (EEF) guidance report, the mechanisms for professional development that have been shown to work globally are clear. As schools and trusts, we need to ask ourselves: do we have the balance right? Are we building teacher knowledge, developing effective techniques, fostering motivation and embedding good practice?

Of course, this isn't easy. We don't need to do everything all at once, nor do we need to implement all 14 of the EEF mechanisms simultaneously. That's not the point. The goal is a balanced, solid and sustained approach to supporting teachers. It's as complex – and as simple – as that.

Writing beyond the school gates

When it comes to writing, I can get quite technical. I can talk about sentence construction, the craft of writing and strategies to improve exam performance. These are pressing realities for every teacher – secondary school teachers are focused on the looming GCSEs, and primary school teachers, particularly those in Year 6, are acutely aware of SATs. These are important considerations and they drive much of the work we do.

But writing has a power that extends far beyond the school gates and that's something we must not lose sight of. This is also a huge opportunity for us as educators – it gives us the energy and motivation to prioritise writing in our teaching. Writing isn't just about succeeding in exams and unlocking the opportunities that follow. It's about self-expression, about finding joy and about communicating with the people we care about. Writing can make us happy, and it can make others happy.

This isn't just procedural practice; it's deeply meaningful work. It matters, not just because it helps pupils achieve academically, but because it equips them with tools for life. Writing enables them to express themselves, connect with others and find fulfilment. What a powerful and rewarding focus for school improvement and leadership.

Questions

John Tomsett (JT): I'm imagining a school leader looking at that shocking drop-off in writing. As a school leader, is there anything we can do? I understand there's no magic bullet, but for those students who need to catch up, what guidance can you give to our colleagues?

Alex Quigley (AQ): For me, it's all about diagnosing the problem. It's not enough to know that a pupil hasn't met the expected standard – what does that actually mean? How far off are they? Did they just miss it by a small margin (and let's be honest, those margins are often arbitrary) or is it a significant gap? This requires good diagnostic assessment, which takes a bit of knowledge about writing to do well. Unlike reading, writing doesn't have a set of national, standardised assessments, so we often need to put in more effort to pinpoint the issues.

I think we can usually trace the problem back to the basics. Writing can be understood through a framework called the **Simple View of Writing**, which includes three key components: transcription, composition and executive function.

1. **Transcription**: this is about the mechanics of handwriting and spelling. Primary school teachers are very aware of the importance of handwriting, but often by Years 2 or 3, we assume pupils have mastered it and stop giving it much attention. However, poor transcription skills – slow handwriting, inaccurate spelling – can hold pupils back significantly. If pupils can't write quickly and accurately, they struggle to get their ideas down in sentences and paragraphs. Diagnostic assessments for handwriting and spelling, such as cumulative spelling tests, can help identify these barriers. For some pupils, focused handwriting practice can make a big difference. Others may need more specialised support. Once we address transcription, we can move on to composition.

2. **Composition**: here, we focus on sentence-level writing. For many pupils, particularly those in Year 5 or Year 7 who are struggling,

the most obvious issue is that they cannot write accurate sentences. Their writing may consist of fragments or poorly punctuated sentences. This is where we need to emphasise modelling sentences, sentence combining and working on sentence structure.

Sentence combining, for example, is a simple but evidence-based strategy. It's particularly effective for pupils with special educational needs. A focused period of practising this skill can help pupils become better writers. It won't magically make them write brilliant stories or essays overnight, but it provides a crucial step forward.

Vocabulary is another key aspect of composition. Pupils with a limited vocabulary often struggle to write with sophistication or creativity. There's no quick fix for this, but we can work on expanding their vocabulary through a rich curriculum. Vocabulary instruction and sentence-level work with synonyms and word choices can make a big difference over time.

3. **Executive function**: this refers to the broader processes involved in writing, such as planning, editing, revising and considering the audience. These are the skills that skilled adult writers use instinctively, but for pupils they need to be explicitly taught. Teachers often assume they're teaching these skills, but when we dig deeper, we find that's not always the case.

   For example, we can teach pupils how to plan effectively, how to edit their work and how to revise thoughtfully. These skills are distinct and should be addressed explicitly. Pupils also need to think about their audience, their language choices and the specific requirements of the task or subject.

So, the Simple View of Writing – transcription, composition and executive function – is where I always start. Every pupil I've worked with who has struggled with writing had issues that could be identified within one or more of these areas. Once we pinpoint the problem, we know where to focus our efforts.

JT: In a primary classroom, what does a writing 'sprint' look like? What do we mean by this?

AQ: A writing 'sprint' is a focused, short burst of practice designed to build specific skills, often at the sentence level. For really young children, one example is **sentence combining**. This involves taking two simple sentences and combining them into one. For instance, if we look at the topic of the Great Fire of London, a useful technique comes from *The Writing Revolution*. The book introduces famous 'signposts' like *because*, *but* and *so*. These connectives are incredibly effective tools for young writers. You might create three sentences where each one uses one of those connectives:

- The fire spread quickly *because* the houses were made of wood.
- The fire was devastating, *but* some buildings were saved.
- The city was rebuilt, *so* it became safer.

Practising with these connectives helps pupils expand their ideas and construct more complex sentences. Over time, this can evolve into building whole paragraphs, particularly with modelling and guidance. As pupils grow older, we introduce more sophisticated connectives and structures. By Year 6, for instance, a pupil might be writing evaluations or more complex explanatory sentences.

Let me give you a specific example. A Year 6 pupil was writing about the Antarctic expedition of *Endurance*. He used the connective 'so that' to structure his reasoning:

- I painted the boat dark blue *so that* it would blend in with the sea.

It's a small tool, but it helps pupils structure their thoughts clearly and purposefully.

For creative writing, a sprint could involve simply expanding a basic sentence. For example:

- **Basic sentence**: He walked down the corridor.
- **Expanded**: He walked cautiously down the dark corridor.

From there, you can add a clause:

- He walked cautiously down the dark corridor, listening for any sound.

53

This iterative process allows pupils to develop their ideas step by step.

It's worth noting that sprints aren't limited to creative writing. In primary school, about half the writing time should focus on developing clear, strong sentences across subjects. For example:

- **In science**: writing clear definitions, like 'Evaporation is when liquid turns into a gas.'
- **In history**: constructing evaluative sentences, such as 'The fire in the bakery was a significant turning point because it led to the rebuilding of London.'

These short, targeted writing exercises are essential. They give pupils regular, focused practice that builds confidence and skill incrementally. If you're interested in more examples, my blog (*The Confident Teacher*) has an upcoming post this Saturday full of ideas for both primary and secondary classrooms.

JT: Alex, are you optimistic about the future of writing?

AQ: It depends. I'm keeping my powder dry, to use an old analogy. There have been some very clear and concerning drops in national outcomes, and those issues don't just go away. You can massage national figures, deprioritise sentence accuracy in science exams or even remove entire national assessments, but the underlying problems remain. There's still a lot of work to be done.

I see a parallel with reading here. Reading and writing are the superpowers we give to our children – skills they should leave school feeling confident in. So while I'm not brimming with optimism, there are reasons to feel hopeful. Teachers are asking the right questions and there's a great deal of interest and energy in addressing the challenges of writing.

As anyone who works in a school knows, people need more support, particularly with specificity and expertise. Too many of us are expected to 'just know' this stuff, but that's not realistic. I certainly didn't have all the answers earlier in my career. If we can provide additional support for teachers and perhaps see some policy changes, then my optimism will grow.

That said, I am always optimistic about what teachers can achieve in the classroom. Teachers have immense potential to make a difference, but they need the right support to do so. Unfortunately, that support isn't always available at the moment.

JT: It's really interesting to think about the path you and I took more than a decade ago. I think we did more personal CPD in the decade between 2010 and 2020 than I did in the first 25 years of my career. But it was all self-driven. What message do you have for school leaders on how they can get themselves up to speed and have meaningful conversations with colleagues about literacy and writing?

AQ: Let's start with the reality we're all facing: recruitment and retention. Before we can focus on professional development, we need to have people in the room to train. We need to reignite demand for teaching as a profession, making it something that graduates are curious about and eager to join. Teaching has to be seen as a desirable, competitive career choice.

Most people who become teachers are driven by a sense of vocation – it's not a job anyone chooses for easy money. But attracting and retaining great teachers isn't just about pay, although that certainly plays a role. It's also about workload, the quality of training and making the profession intellectually stimulating. Post-Covid, many careers now offer flexibility and opportunities for remote working, so teaching needs to stand out as a fulfilling, attractive option.

Part of what keeps people in the profession – and attracts them to it in the first place – is the promise of high-quality professional development. Once we have people in the room, it's about creating a sustainable rhythm of professional development. This requires a tricky balancing act: focusing on fewer, narrower areas rather than trying to do everything at once. Throwing everything at the wall and hoping something sticks doesn't work. Instead, we need to engage with the mechanisms of effective professional development and sustain those efforts over time.

I've learned a lot about CPD since my time leading it. For instance, one key insight is the importance of practising techniques outside of lessons. Teachers need time and space to refine their skills collaboratively before applying them in the classroom. This aligns with the guidance around professional development and is something school leaders need to champion.

Being brave as a leader means identifying specific, narrow areas of focus for professional development and sticking with them. Think about the analogy of sprints and marathons: CPD plans and school improvement strategies need to be streamlined to allow sustained engagement with one or two challenging problems at a time.

One of the big positives I see, especially in England, is the enormous engagement with research and evidence. School leaders here are engaging with research-informed practice and networks at a world-leading level. This provides a strong foundation for improvement. However, these leaders need support to make CPD truly effective. If we can hold our nerve, focus on a few key priorities, and deliver sustained, high-quality training, we can make a real and lasting difference.

Chapter 7
Leadership 55 wisdom – teaching and learning

Your title is head*teacher*. If you're a headteacher today, now, in 2025, when it comes to teaching and learning you have enormous support to aid your understanding of which teaching techniques best help students learn. Indeed, knowledge of how children learn and how to shape teaching to engender learning is better than it has ever been since the school system began. Truly.

Near the end of my school career, I used to do a talk called '25 years of hurt'. Looking back, my PGCE training was poor. Consequently, I taught for a quarter of a century without really knowing what I was doing – I got by on force of character and sheer enthusiasm. Students enjoyed the lessons. They were engaged. GCSE and A-level results were pretty good. But looking back, it could have been so much better. Only in the last 12 years of my career, since I learned so much about teaching and learning, did I begin to employ teaching strategies that had the best chance of helping students learn.

So, when I was first a headteacher, I didn't know what I didn't know about teaching and learning. I was 'a feather for each wind that blows'. I was Dylan Wiliam's magpie, made real – a snapper-up of myriad shiny teaching and learning techniques, which one training course after another said would transform examination outcomes overnight.

Some elements of the KS3 Strategy were useful and have stood the test of time. Dylan Wiliam's *Inside the Black Box* came out the same week in 1998 that I began as a deputy at Huntington and I even bothered to ring Dylan to chat about it with him. I have heard him repeat what he said to me during our phone call on that autumn morning in 1998 at conferences over the last three decades. But when I became responsible for everything in a school on 1 September 2003, I hardly knew anything about teaching and learning.

The thing is it is easy to make token gestures to help you feel like you are doing something. In my first headship, we bought every teacher a copy of Paul Ginnis's tremendous book *The Teacher's Toolkit*. It was a big deal. The book is great if you use it judiciously over several years and work on one or two elements of practice you need to improve. Just throwing books at teachers and thinking that is all you need to do will do *diddly squat* to improve teaching. Goodness knows how much that initiative cost us and goodness knows where those books are now…

Looking back, I don't reckon that gesture of largesse had any impact whatsoever on the quality of teaching and learning. But it made me feel a bit better. I could tell governors that we had bought books and had had a whole training session launching the initiative. What I didn't tell governors was that there was no follow-through at all on the *Teacher's Toolkit* initiative, just an after-school launch session. The thing is I didn't know I was being so rubbish.

If I had my time again, I would have done things very differently. So, here are my top five tips for headteachers for *establishing a position on teaching and learning*:

1. **To begin with, read some essential publications on teaching and learning.** There have been more books on teaching and learning published in the last ten years than you can possibly find time to read. However, if you feel like you need to get up to speed so you have a position on teaching and learning, this admittedly subjective selection will help enormously:

    - Daniel Willingham's *Why Don't Students Like School?*
    - Dylan Wiliam and Paul Black's *Inside the Black Box*
    - Graham Nuthall's *The Hidden Lives of Learners*
    - Tom Sherrington's *The Learning Rainforest*
    - Daisy Christodoulou's *Making Good Progress?*
    - Barbara Oakley's *Learning How to Learn*
    - Tom Sherrington and Oliver Caviglioli's *WalkThrus* series
    - Mary Myatt's *Huh* curriculum series (co-written with me)
    - Mary Myatt's *The Curriculum: Gallimaufry to Coherence*
    - Héctor Ruiz Martín's *How Do We Learn? A Scientific Approach to Learning and Teaching*
    - Barak Rosenshine's *Principles of Instruction* (or Tom Sherrington's brilliant explanation of the principles)
    - Adam Boxer's *Explicit & Direct Instruction*
    - Dylan Wiliam's introduction to the National Curriculum.

    As a headteacher I think you have to take responsibility for your own professional development, and these publications are a great start. You have to know what you are talking about. And to keep you up to date there are so many good resources online. People like Tom Sherrington, Harry Fletcher-Wood, Kate Jones, Adam Boxer, Mary Myatt, Jade Pearce, David Didau, Bradley Busch, Carl Hendrick, Peps Mccrea, Ruth Ashbee, Sarah Cottinghatt, Alex Quigley, Christine Counsell, the Education Endowment Foundation, Deans for Impact *and so many more* are publishing their ideas on a daily basis.

2. **If you need to, sort out behaviour before you do anything else in school.** Until you have good student behaviour in lessons right

across your school, you cannot focus upon developing teaching and learning. You may never get student behaviour perfect in every lesson, every day, but you have to establish consistently good student behaviour before your colleagues can begin the challenging work of improving their teaching.

3. **Watch everyone teach.** Be ruthless. Once behaviour is sorted out, make this a priority. And emphasise that you want to see *everyday* lessons, nothing fancy. No *speed camera* lessons. Just what we do in our classrooms, day in, day out. Look at what pupils are learning as much as at what teachers are doing. Feedback swiftly and dialogically. No judgements, just have a discussion about what people think about teaching and why they choose to teach the way they do. Reflect upon what you have learned and engage in professional conversations about teaching and learning frequently, both formally and informally. But, remember, you can only do that if you know what you are talking about. This process will help you understand what needs to be done to improve the quality of teaching and learning in the school you are leading, in its context. And show wilful humility, something Jim Collins defines as 'tremendous ambition for your school combined with the stoic will to do whatever it takes, to make the school great. Yet at the same time display a remarkable humility about yourself, ascribing much of your own success to luck, discipline and preparation rather than personal genius.'

4. **Prioritise professional development.** Tom Bentley said at an NCTL conference in 1996 that 'once you have found your core purpose, change your school's existing structures to accommodate your core purpose rather than accommodate your core purpose around your existing structures'. The development of teaching and learning is your priority. In essence, find the hours during the school week for your staff to work on their practice. You must not expect them to do it all in their own time. And any logistical barrier can be overcome. Just because half your students come to school on buses does not mean you cannot finish early once a fortnight for training: just sort it out with the bus companies and with your parents. No logistical barrier should stop you in improving the quality of teaching and learning.

5. **As a minimum, aim for everyone to understand the relationship between curriculum content, adaptive teaching and assessment.** If you accomplished that, it would be an enormous step forward. Once that is clear in everyone's mind, you can begin to shape a professional training and development programme, which is tailored around the needs of each subject area in your school, something that will take you five years to mature. You might need to begin with curriculum content, or it might be that you need to focus on the teaching of domain-specific vocabulary, or you may need to reset the assessment regime. Whatever it is, do not overwhelm colleagues. If everything else remains the same in your school's classrooms from one year to the next, but you improve *one* major element of teaching and learning over that time, genuinely and deeply, then you will have a significantly better school. Do that over five years and you will have transformed the school.

Remember, it's one step at a time.

Chapter 8
A conversation on diversity with Bennie Kara

My section is on the leadership of diversity, equity and inclusion (DEI). I want to begin by saying that this is an emerging field of leadership. I have observed an increase in the number of DEI leadership posts in schools. This rise is partly due to the growing emphasis on pupil voice, on the experiences of individuals, not just in terms of the curriculum, but also their sense of belonging within schools. This focus has become prominent in questions from Ofsted. However, it is not solely driven by Ofsted; it reflects a broader recognition of an area that has been historically neglected. Since there is now a directive to address protected characteristics in the curriculum, we are starting to see more leaders emerging in this field.

One common issue I find in DEI leadership is the sense that it is a 'fluffy' role, often appointed based on passion. While passion is necessary for functioning in this space, it is often assumed that DEI leaders focus on personal or interpersonal activities. The terms bandied around about DEI leaders are 'someone who is empathetic', 'someone who can be a confidant, coach or mentor', or at the very least an advocate. This narrow view limits the understanding of DEI leadership. It should be regarded as a more rigorous endeavour, akin to any other aspect of school improvement, requiring a combination of various skills.

Fundamentally, this work involves change management and leadership of people who may or may not be on board with these changes. Whether the change pertains to curriculum, assessment or pastoral care, a DEI leader needs to be analytical and able to architect the necessary structures within a school. This role is not just about one individual but about a team with a shared vision, building something significant. Within that process, there will be challenges. Some schools may lose focus on DEI due to the difficulty of the work or staff turnover, particularly if it is not embedded into the system.

Like any other leadership endeavour, DEI work requires an iterative approach, from planning to implementation to evaluation. I often turn to the EEF implementation framework as a valuable guide in this process. DEI work lies at the intersection of being and doing. While being empathetic, an advocate and a mentor is very important, the doing part is the most challenging. The ideal DEI leader understands those needs of 'being' but also understands the need for architecture and planning to take place.

Reflecting on this, regardless of your specific leadership role, consider how much you exist in that middle between being and doing. We often talk about the qualities of a leader and the plans that need to be made, but sometimes the golden thread is somewhere in the middle. When appointing someone to, or encouraging someone in, this role, it's important to make them aware that, like any school project and management, it is crucial.

Conditions for change

One of the first things to consider as a leader in this field is the conditions needed to implement any change. I was reading an interesting article in *The Guardian* about artificial grass. I know that sounds boring, but it talked about how artificial grass would survive a nuclear apocalypse. While I do carry a deep-seated hatred for artificial grass, it made me think about school conditions. Look at the difference between artificial grass and real grass. Artificial grass, which looks pristine and requires no maintenance, represents an unrealistic approach to DEI or any change management. Real grass, which is patchy and requires care, represents the true conditions necessary for DEI work. Identifying and addressing these needs allows us to sow the seeds for genuine growth. Excuse the continual gardening metaphors, but the real grass has space for planting new things and gaps that need filling.

The conditions in your school around DEI need careful handling because there will be some people who are on board and recognise the need for it, some people who think about it as a tick-box activity, and there are some people who will actively resist it. Gauging the mood for change is a huge part of starting any process. So, how do we create those conditions? We look for gaps and areas where things need to be planted. This requires an element of realism because you can't plant things where they're not needed or where there isn't enough space. Sometimes there are things you can remove to make space, but ultimately, when it comes to race, disability, sexuality, gender and other protected characteristics, it's about working out what is already in place, what is missing, and what are the priorities. Doing it all at once is a fool's endeavour. You cannot implement teaching and leadership around nine protected characteristics plus potential intersectionality without considering your context, your children, the community, the parents, and the age and stage of your children. What happens at primary, for example, might be very different from what happens at secondary.

Planning

The second element is the planning stage. This stage, when I've worked with schools across the country, has been the most useful part because through careful planning, schools can identify strengths and gaps, ensuring the necessary skills, resources and time are allocated to DEI work. It takes a very focused mind to be able to sit down and meticulously map out what it will look like.

I often find with DEI initiatives and leadership in this area that the need to do something quickly transforms into trying to do everything. Prioritisation, having people with the necessary skills and ensuring there is money and time built into the system to do this work – these aspects often get lost. The planning, while initially done individually, needs to then be submitted to others for a critical eye. Stakeholder voice becomes part of this process as people contribute to your plans. Much of this work is about persuasion and influence rather than just composing documents or improvement plans. Your initial plans might be very different from the final ones, and that's okay because we add and remove things as we develop our processes.

It's important to note the high project failure rate often discussed in industry. Approximately 70% of projects fail and this is probably true in schools as well. There's often significant enthusiasm at the beginning of a project, but poor planning can lead to long-term failure. Unrealistic deadlines, lack of time or budget, and resistance can cause knee-jerk reactions and result in surface-level work. We are aiming for depth work involving curriculum, pastoral systems, student voice and community engagement. Without proper planning and realism, measuring progress becomes difficult, and this work requires measurable impact, whether qualitative or quantitative. Planning for that measurement – what the project is going to look like at given points in time – is crucial.

Projects also often fail because one person has been the linchpin. If that person moves on or priorities shift, the project can be put on the backburner. Therefore, it cannot be a solo effort. That kind of hero leadership, while predicated on personality and passion, must also involve building capacity within the team to ensure sustainability.

Effective communication and bringing people on board are crucial. Think about the roles of the people around you, both up and down the hierarchy. I often refer to Belbin team roles to determine who will fulfil certain spaces. If you take on all roles as a leader, you will burn out. Identify who are the thinkers, the doers and the evaluators. Leverage the strengths of those willing to engage with the research and those who are doers.

Mapping this out with people's names can be helpful. Consider succession planning: who will take over if you leave? Ensure that the initiative is sustainable and part of the school's fabric, not just a one-off project.

Projects often fail due to inadequate planning. Effective DEI leadership requires setting realistic deadlines, ensuring sufficient resources, and planning for measurable outcomes. It is essential to embed this work into the school's fabric, moving beyond a single individual's efforts to a sustainable, systemic approach.

Agility

As a leader, you need to be able to adapt, change direction and not panic. Agility is essential. Good leadership involves anticipating blocks, navigating difficult spaces and knowing who is on your side. Be prepared to replan and redirect efforts as needed. This agile mindset is common in the business world and involves understanding your work environment and whom you're working with.

Leverage the people around you, understand their power and interest, and keep them informed. The more interested and powerful someone is, the more you need to keep them engaged. Some people might not have done the research, so keep them informed to engage and consult them as critical friends.

Agility also means being honest with yourself, constantly evaluating and anticipating potential barriers. This hazard perception is crucial because if you anticipate issues, you are better prepared. Agility is key for any leader, especially within the DEI space.

Finally, keep in mind the national landscape and the politicisation of DEI issues. A good leader in this space stays informed about ongoing conversations and their implications.

Voice

I want to talk a little bit about voice. I think we underestimate voice – student voice, staff voice, parent voice, community voice – because it feels like something that you do as an add-on for, perhaps, the inspector, as opposed to something you do to guide you through a process or any kind of project.

The most powerful conversations I have had when I'm consulting around DEI in schools are when I sit down with the children. I ask them a series of questions, very simple things like 'What does diversity mean on a really basic level?' And then I ask them what their experiences are in school and I see teachers saying, 'Hang on! We didn't know that.' That might be simply because they've never been asked the questions before.

So much of the work around voice, I think, is done more powerfully face to face. You may also want to include a facilitator, because what children say to their regular teachers is not necessarily what they'll say to an external person. Actually, some schools' movements into a category have been due to students sharing very concerning things that happen in school that they believe aren't being dealt with. Where are we giving them the opportunity to have that conversation? And not just sticking to the basics – 'Do you experience racism? Do you experience homophobia?' – but actually asking them about gender-based violence and misogyny, and how is masculinity dealt with? Sometimes this is done only partially.

While on the one side we have student voice, staff voice is equally important. I've been in situations where I've delivered training to schools, and staff members have stood up and said they've experienced racism in school and never had an opportunity to say that before. Considering this as a wellbeing activity is part of the role, not just as a coach or mentor, but to feed into your evaluation process and the analytics you're putting out for the people who need to know, and for yourself.

Parent voice, meanwhile, is harder to leverage. Some people find it unhelpful or they perceive it to be unhelpful. I think that's because there is a fear that what's out in the community might not align with the values of the school. That's a very real fear for people in this space.

Ultimately, there's a very soft and very gentle approach that probably needs to be taken around asking small groups of parents to engage with some of the issues and bringing in parents who have those protected characteristics first. After that, you need to think about who you need to persuade in the wider community.

The conflict often comes around LGBT and religion. That is one of the driving fears for many DEI leaders. If we advocate for LGBT children and staff, how will that clash with religious communities be navigated? When you've gathered these voices, you need to be able to say: these are our values and this is who we are – you make a choice when you come to our school. That's often how I state it.

Then tap into community voice. Who are your community leaders with power and influence? Think about people with high levels of knowledge around the area, but also power within communities to enact change. Have you brought them in? Who are your imams, your chaplains, your youth groups who work with specific communities? Have you talked to them about this space? Can you use them to have conversations with your stakeholders?

Because if we don't listen as leaders, nothing happens; everything is in a vacuum. Having these voices allows you to go back to that plan. It's part of a process: you might get that staff voice, then replan, re-evaluate and go through the steps as you proceed.

Knowledge

One of the last things I want to talk about is your own knowledge. People often ask me: how do you know this stuff if you don't have one of those protected characteristics? And I often say, well, I didn't know how to teach Dickens until I learned how to teach Dickens. I'm an unashamedly voracious reader!

The key role for any leader, but particularly in this space, is to think of yourself as a reader/researcher. Keeping abreast of the issues isn't just important on a national level; it can also expand to an international level. Some of the books and texts I've read come from different countries and contexts but are applicable in a UK setting.

As a DEI leader, your role is to be the conduit for information. People will ask you how they can know *what they don't know*. Initially, there's the need to broker information and provide signposts for problematic areas. Be confident enough to say, 'I know you don't have time to read a whole book, but here's a snippet or an article I want you to cover.'

My organisation, Diverse Educators, which I co-founded with Hannah Wilson, has been collating information into bite-sized toolkits for people to tap into. There are Padlets around diversity in the curriculum because people often don't have time to do everything. Using these resources and being that kind of information broker will increase people's confidence in you.

Any leader is a model for learning. A leader must tap into crucial conversations, particularly around politicised topics like LGBT issues. You need to know what is being said out there. There are times when it can be a cesspit, but I get a lot of my information from social media because I can triangulate it with my own research.

Recognising that you don't need to reinvent the wheel is essential. We often tell early career teachers not to plan from scratch; this is the same. See what's out there – there are schemes of work and programmes in place. Assessing the landscape allows you to enlist your own sources of support, which is a form of research in itself. Then you'll be able to triangulate what you're doing with what other places are doing. That may or may not fit your context, but if it does, it's a win.

The fundamental part of this role is finding yourself in a servant leadership position. As a reader and researcher, you're there to support others in doing their job because you're not doing it alone. Hero leadership wears people out and isn't sustainable in the long term.

John Tomsett (JT): You talked about measuring DEI. What kind of measures are there for evaluating success?

Bennie Kara (BK): Quite often this comes in the form of voice. You gather initial views about DEI in a particular context and then what that looks like after a certain amount of time has passed and certain measures have been implemented. We talk a lot in this space about how exactly to measure it. Often it is based on what children say about their curriculum, what they say about pastoral systems and what comes up in parent surveys for Ofsted. Those are the basic measurements.

But it might also involve teacher efficacy. When measuring teacher progress in terms of their development, do you have something built into your teaching and learning criteria that you can measure? In a school I worked in, we had a section that said: 'Celebrates diversity and challenges discrimination in any form'. We start with an initial figure of qualitative data, provide the training and then review it regularly. During curriculum planning, we assess whether the curriculum has shifted effectively. I do a lot of work on curriculum development, ensuring it's not just tokenistic but enriches and enhances the curriculum in a logical, sequential way that fosters conversations across phases and stages.

When we try to pin it down to numbers, the biggest test is staff and student retention, particularly among specific groups. It might also involve looking at attendance rates for our LGBT children and incidences of homophobic or racist bullying. Having markers in place and matching the data with the work you're doing allows you to demonstrate the impact. Then it becomes not just about one particular aspect; it's about holistic impact: this figure shows it, this story tells it, this parent says it. When people come through the door and say they feel really welcome here, that's a measurement of impact.

Chapter 9
Leadership 55 wisdom – being patient

Headteachers usually assume that they arrive at a school and have to make their mark. Schools are notoriously vulnerable in the wake of regime change. A new headteacher can lead to a significant modification of the values and educational philosophy of a school. And perfectly good systems are suddenly abandoned for the new boss's favoured alternatives, without a shred of evidence that in this new setting their old favourites will work. So, out goes setting, in comes mixed prior attainment; goodbye SIMS, hello Bromcom; exit Year Groups, enter Houses. And the rest of the staff just have to suck it up and watch while what worked stops working…

The context of each headship is different and each requires a different leadership style. School boards appoint according to context. If a school is in some turmoil, then the governing body will usually want a seasoned leader who can act decisively; conversely, a school that is bobbing along quite nicely is more likely to appoint a first-time leader who can take their time in shaping the school.

New headteachers have lots of onlookers tracking their every move. They have myriad voices trying to influence them, telling them several different versions of the school and how it works. They feel pressured to do something that changes the direction of the school. That pressure builds. Instinctively, they want to make their mark, which is understandable but misguided.

What many resort to is a change in the school uniform. Such a step requires a significant time investment and achieves little. The first day I stood on the main corridor as a headteacher I called over a girl called Sarah and told her politely that her tailored shirt, with three-quarter sleeves and no top button, would have to be changed. She also looked like she had just ram-raided Ratner's the jewellers.

Sarah, in turn, politely pointed out that every other girl in the corridor was wearing the same style of shirt and was similarly bejewelled. There then ensued a six-month process of uniform change, during which I managed to upset the whole school community. And I also stopped Year 10 going into town for lunch. That made the front page of the local newspaper.

I felt confused but desperate to appear proactive. I didn't know which battles to pick. I instigated a move to a faculty system, solely on the recommendation of a local authority adviser. The faculty system introduced another expensive tier of leadership – we retained subject leader posts within the faculty structure(!?!) – without improving the quality of teaching at all. But I was doing things. I appeared incredibly busy. By the end of my first year, I felt exhausted and isolated. I had upset people without moving the school on at all.

We had a full Ofsted inspection eight days into that first headship: 16 inspectors for four days. It was a perfectly timed review of the school and gave me a blueprint for improvement. My fruitless 'activity-for-the-sake-of-it' stopped early in my second year when we began focusing upon the quality of teaching, as the Ofsted report had suggested we should do. We also began tracking students' progress more accurately.

We refrained from doing things peripheral to improving what was going on in the classroom.

My four-year-long first headship saw the school move from 38th out of 47 schools in North Yorkshire for KS2–KS4 progress, to 3rd out of 47 schools. But I learned the hard way; the whole process wore me thin. When I began my second headship, I was the epitome of patience. We drew up a ten-year plan and, while we did not follow the plan to the letter, we hit every milestone at the right time; ten years later, Ofsted popped in, almost unannounced, and declared we were outstanding'.

Such long-term planning can seem impossible for the headteacher who feels the need to do things immediately. But if they can resist such pressure and be patient, it will turn out best for the school – and for them personally – over time. So, if you are appointed to lead a school and feel compelled to introduce blazers with gold braiding on the lapels, just to look like you are doing something, here are my top five tips for headteachers for being patient:

1. **Explain to your chair of the school board that you intend to be patient** and that they should not expect significant change anytime soon. Explain your timeline for change over the first three years.
2. **Spend your first term getting to know the school.** Speak to everyone. Be about the place. Question what everyone says. Analyse performance data. Triangulate. Then over the Christmas holidays, formulate your own version of the truth about the school, based on the most robust evidence. Then take a day with your senior team and go through a process with them to establish their truth about the school compared with yours, so that, by the end of the day, you agree as a whole team the current state of the school and the one or two things that need to be done, when and how, in order to improve the school.
3. **Be careful what you say.** When I had been appointed to my first headship, a York headteacher said to me, 'Be careful of what you say because people will remember it and quote it back to you months, even years, down the line.' And he was dead right.
4. **It is the best ideas for improvement that count most, not yours.** Have the confidence to develop others in your team and give

them the chance to accept responsibility and accountability for their improvement initiatives. Leadership is best measured in the leadership you develop in others.

5. **In the first instance, focus on teaching and learning.** You have to build from the bottom up, starting in the classroom. Support your frontline staff. Have conversations about teaching with everyone who teaches in your school. And no matter how busy you might be, you must teach *really well*. Be patient; you teaching well matters more than you might ever realise.

Chapter 10
A conversation on instructional coaching with Jim Knight

It's going to be a bit of a challenge to give a brief explanation of instructional coaching, because we have a 16-week course that meets every week for three and a half hours, as well as 12 books on the subject. So there's a lot to cover. However, having to be brief will force me to try to be concise, and that may not be a bad thing.

I have developed a Venn diagram for coaching consisting of the following areas: the 'way of being' behind the coaching as we describe it, the coaching process, the coaching skills and strategic knowledge. Here I'll particularly focus on 'way of being' and the coaching process.

By way of introduction, let me say a little bit about where the idea of instructional coaching came from. I was teaching English in Toronto, Canada, and was doing doctoral studies in English at the University of Toronto. But my plans changed – my wife and I had two kids in one year, 362 days apart, so, suddenly I needed to get a job and make money.

I started teaching at a community college. I thought I was going to teach Shakespeare, 'the modern novel' or something like that, but I ended up teaching special ed. I didn't even know what a learning disability was and didn't know what to do. Luckily, a colleague, Dee La France, offered to help. She trained me in a model called the strategic instruction model. I liked it and was successful at using it. In fact, my course got an award and I got a full-time job.

I came to Kansas from Toronto. I got certified as a professional developer and started to do training (that was the word we would use) around Southern Ontario. The evaluations of the trainings were nice, but there was zero implementation; no change at all.

Recognising that improvement was needed, I turned to Michael Fullan, who was teaching at the University of Toronto at the time. He was very generous with his time: I did an independent study with him and took a course from him – he's still my mentor in many ways. Later, I decided to pursue my doctorate at the University of Kansas, which was then, and continues to be, highly regarded for its special education programme.

We received a lot of funding for research on coaching, over $30 million over 15 years. We started out with a concept called 'learning consulting'. However, I decided that the term was too hierarchical, so we shifted to 'instructional collaborator'. I still wasn't pleased with it and eventually arrived at 'instructional coach' and first used the term in an article for the *Journal of Staff Development*.

A couple years later, I wrote *Instructional Coaching*, which was the first book with the term 'instructional coaching' on its cover. This may not sound very revolutionary today, but up to that time, I had never met somebody calling themselves an instructional coach who didn't work for us. So, imagine my surprise when one day I was at a professional development conference in the United States and heard someone say, 'Well, I'm an instructional coach.' I'll never forget it. Now, on LinkedIn, there are close to 100,000 people who identify themselves as instructional coaches.

When I started as a professional developer, I felt like my job was to describe practices really effectively and emphasise the importance of fidelity of implementation. But I could feel during the sessions that something wasn't working. This idea of me telling professionals what to do wasn't effective. The teachers in our workshops would thank us for the materials, they'd say it was a good idea, but then they put the books on their shelves and never used them again.

The idea that one person has all the expertise and the other person is ignorant and has to be told what to do is both dehumanising and ineffective. Telling people what to do is not an evidence-based model for change – it's probably not going to work. In the moment, you might feel like you have valuable things to say, but if you come back and you check a year later, you're probably not going to see sustained change.

Therefore, I started to read widely about change in areas such as cultural anthropology, organisational behaviour, organisational leadership, educational theory, sociology and psychology, and eventually developed a set of principles called the Partnership Principles, which reflect the first circle in the Venn diagram, the 'way of being'.

The way of being

Based on my reading, and ultimately the research we did, I came to the conclusion that the conversations we have about learning should be what Paulo Freire calls 'mutually humanising conversations'. This, in turn, led me to develop what I call the Partnership Principles. Here are a few of the core ideas behind them.

Choice stands at the heart of what we do, and that helps engender this idea of a mutually humanising conversation, where both partners are empowered – grounded in humility on the part of the coach, openness to hearing the other person's opinions, faith in the other person and the belief that they can succeed, and an attitude of benevolence. The coach should be genuinely interested in what's good for the teacher and what's good for the students. It's not about the coach; it's about the teacher.

A number of other things also go into this way of being and the partnership approach, but fundamentally we're flipping the way we do professional development. Traditionally, what happens is that an expert on practice shows up at the school with, for example, ideas from research on feedback and instructs the staff to implement it. There might even be some kind of follow-up, including implementation practice.

However, working from what we call the partnership perspective, we've gone in the completely opposite direction. We don't start with a given practice. We start with what the kids need. Then we figure out a change in engagement or achievement we want to accomplish – one the teacher really cares about. The teacher identifies that goal and then we work backwards: now that we have a goal, we set about to figure out a strategy that is needed to accomplish the goal. We found when you start with kids instead of starting with a strategy, it ends up boosting rates of implementation. In one of our studies, we had an effect size of 1.02, which is pretty high.

When we used the partnership approach, people were four and a half times more likely to plan to implement than when we took a more directive approach. And we accomplish the same things: a coach *should* have expertise, but using the partnership approach they don't act like an expert, they act like a partner. They start by asking questions, helping the other person set the goal.

For example, if the teacher suggests something that won't have a positive impact on kids, or at least doesn't sound like a wise decision to the coach, the coach might say, 'Do you mind if I share some thoughts I have about this?' That is, in the partnership approach, we position the teacher as the decision-maker because the reality is that the teacher *is* the decision-maker. But also it's dehumanising for the teacher to not have a choice. Choice is what defines us, and as Peter Block says, 'If we cannot say "no", then "yes" has no meaning.' So that's the coaching 'way of being'.

The coaching process

The second part of the Venn diagram is the coaching process. How do you live out the beliefs in the 'way of being'? I want to be clear: I'm not saying we don't share ideas; we just share ideas in a way that honours the professional discretion of the teachers with whom we work. We feel that to have the schools we want, we need teachers who are professionals, and professionals have discretion. Professionals don't just follow a universal script. If you go see a surgeon or general practitioner or architect, for example, they're going to use their brain to make special decisions about your particular situation. Given that, using a research approach we call 'lean design research' – a combination of the book *The Lean Startup* and everything we know about design research – we did multiple iterations with coaches in Oregon and Washington and continually refined our coaching model until we arrived at the process we call the Impact Cycle.

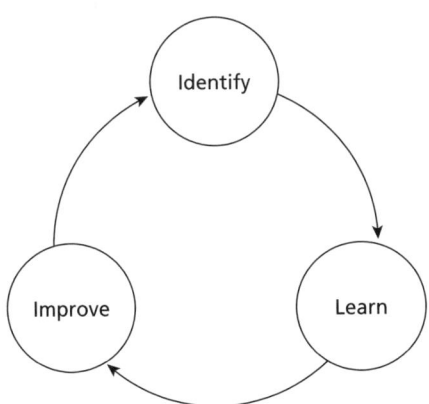

Within the Impact Cycle, we first *identify* a clear picture of reality, then an emotionally compelling student-focused goal the teacher wants to achieve, and finally help the teacher *learn* a method or a strategy to reach that goal. We then help the teacher to *improve* by clearly describing the strategy but simultaneously allowing the teacher to modify it to make it work in their classroom.

As part of the process, often the teacher sees the practice or observes another teacher perform it. They may co-teach with the coach, or the coach might come into the classroom. The teacher might even watch a video of the strategy. The point is the teacher hears about a practice, has a clear explanation of it (probably using a checklist) and sees it modelled for them. Then they can modify it to make it work for them in their own classroom.

If a teacher were to say, 'I want to brutalise this teaching practice. I want to do it in a way that nobody thinks would work,' the coach would say, 'Well, you know your kids better than I do. You know how you teach. But let me tell you what I think, and then you make a decision.' Don't forget, they have a goal, so their primary target is that goal, and the goal is the objective standard for excellence. The rigorous model for excellent instruction is: did it actually change kids?

We found that telling teachers what to do isn't likely to change much of what happens in the classroom. There are many reasons for this. Sometimes, once we implement a new strategy, we find it doesn't work. For example, we have a goal and we measure changes in students to see progress toward that goal, but sometimes the things we identify have to be adapted. Sometimes we have the wrong strategy. Sometimes we have the wrong goal. Sometimes the way we're implementing the strategy needs to be modified.

As Ron Heifetz at Harvard says, 'When you face adaptive challenges, you need adaptive solutions.' The improve stage in the cycle is where you adapt your methods and strategies to make them work for kids. Telling people what to do assumes a 'one-size-fits-all' situation. We don't think 'one size fits all' makes sense in education. Given the complexities of the classroom, it's more appropriate to say 'one size fits one'. Therefore, we emphasise that coaches and teachers have to adapt to make it work.

More often than not in a coaching situation, what teachers were doing may not have been very effective. That means, as a coach, you must have a clear idea of teaching practices – that's where what we call an instructional playbook comes in. Coaches need to develop a core of 15 or 20 strategies that they know – high-impact strategies with evidence-based backing – and they also need to be skilled at gathering data so they can set goals and monitor progress. Those goals should be based around engagement and achievement.

Coaching skills

The third part is coaching skills. These are universal coaching skills: the way you ask questions and the way you listen. First off, if the teacher you're talking to says they don't feel they've been heard, they are most likely right. When you listen effectively, people should know. This is manifested in what you do externally and internally, and it's also about treating the person with respect. Honour teachers as professionals; it's not a case of 'I'm one up, and I'm going to tell them what to do.' In a coaching conversation, *two professionals* are having a respectful, dialogical conversation. Therefore, the way a coach listens and asks questions is very important.

A good listener is effective both internally and externally. *Internally* they must stay focused on what the other person is saying and not get distracted by their own assumptions. The trouble is that talk is slower than our brains move, so to be a good listener, we almost always need to slow our brain down. *Externally* a good listener turns towards the other person and makes an appropriate amount of eye contact – too much can be off-putting. They also avoid interrupting the person when they're talking. Nancy Kline has written about this. Additionally, a good listener lets the speaker answer the question in their own time. Susan Scott sums this up well in the following quotation: 'When we really ask, people really listen, and somehow both of us are validated.' That's what we're really striving for – a conversation where the other person feels more efficacious, more effective, more intelligent and more capable. This doesn't happen when there's a hierarchical dynamic because it makes one person feel diminished.

Strategic knowledge

The last aspect is essential knowledge. What makes instructional coaching different from, say, Sir John Whitmore's approach, Nancy Kline's approach or the idea of 'growth coaching' that my friend Christian van Nieuwerburgh is an expert in, is that instructional coaches have specific knowledge about instruction and the classroom that informs their work. They have a playbook and know what effective teaching practices look like. They've spent time identifying the highest-leverage strategies to help teachers hit their goals. I would say it's better for the coach to know a small number of strategies really well than to know many strategies superficially. To achieve quality implementation, professional development must go beyond the conceptual level – it's about rigorous application.

In addition to a depth of knowledge, instructional coaches need to know how to gather data on engagement and achievement. A lot of work has been done on how to use data effectively. Data, when used correctly, should foster hope and reveal insights that wouldn't otherwise be apparent, as it examines each student in the classroom. Data need to be gathered frequently and iteratively so you can see if what you're doing is working. That is how you assess effectiveness: if the strategy you're using has zero impact on learning, engagement, or the wellbeing of kids, it's not working! Without measurement, you can't claim a strategy is effective. The effectiveness of strategies is the impact they have on kids.

Conclusion

If you look at the body of literature on effective instruction, you'll find varying opinions. Bryan Goodwin's rigorous assessment of teaching practices differs from John Hattie's meta-analyses, which, in turn, differ from what Marzano said, and Tom Sherrington has yet another perspective. Through instructional coaching, we focus on local validity: did the data show that it worked? That's how we know it works.

To summarise, we work from a partnership perspective – the so-called 'way of being'. We also have a cycle called the Impact Cycle, we have coaching skills and we have strategic knowledge. Within this approach, the coach has expertise but doesn't act like an expert. They act like a teacher talking to a teacher. The conversation between a coach and a teacher should feel exactly the same as the conversations they would have had before one of them became a coach.

Using this approach, we're flipping the way professional development has traditionally been done. That is, instead of starting with the strategy and trying to force it to fit in our classrooms, we start with an emotionally compelling goal, knowing that if the teacher doesn't care about the goal, it won't happen. We ask, 'What are your students not doing now that you'd like to see them do?' We use video to get a clearer picture of the classroom reality. Finally, once we have an emotionally compelling goal that the teacher is committed to and that will unmistakably positively impact kids, we use our knowledge about effective instruction to identify the strategies that can help us reach the goal. And that's the whole purpose: to significantly improve the quality of children's lives.

I'm passionate about this work, as we all are about helping kids. The most important thing is to keep doing what works, but don't guess – know if it's working. There are many pathways to successful students, and this is just one of them.

Questions

John Tomsett (JT): Instructional coaching, the way you described it, is very focused on the interpersonal approach that the coach takes with the teacher. Sometimes, in the UK, it seems that the instructional playbook plays a more important role, because those are kind of the practices that the coach or head of school wants to see in the classroom. What do you think about that kind of emphasis put on the playbook?

Jim Knight (JK): There is a better approach than focusing on the playbook and it involves seeing teachers as professionals. It's better to give teachers a voice and a choice, and to start with changes in students. Our evidence is clear on this. There is so much you can lose if you simply tell people what to do.

Of course, if something is working, keep doing it – every situation is different. It could be that a charismatic leader at your school can drive change effectively, but the danger is that when that person leaves, their charisma goes with them, and the organisation may revert to its previous state.

We advocate for a laser-like focus, not on conversation or teachers, but on doing what's best for students. So we begin by asking, 'What's the change we need to see in students?' Instructional coaches must have a deep understanding of instructional practices and know the playbook. However, we don't start with the strategy; we start with the change we want to see in students. This means focusing on something powerful, even if it's not what I, as the observer, think is the most important. John Campbell, the founder of Growth Coaching in Australia, says, 'A less-than-perfect goal chosen by the teacher is better than the perfect goal chosen by the coach.'

Research by Edgar Schein, Deci and Ryan, Miller and Rollnick, and Dan Pink's book *Drive* all support this notion: if you don't care about the goal, you won't reach it. So you have to start with the students. That inevitably leads to an emotionally compelling goal. I've seen many teachers try to implement what they've been told to do, but within a year, they revert back to their old ways. They might have objectives written on the board, but they're not committed to them.

I feel strongly about this based on our research. Ten or 15 years ago, my approach to coaching was telling teachers what to do. But we gradually learned that we were not achieving quality implementation. Through using our 'lean design research', mentioned earlier, with coaches in different settings, we realised that change must start with the students.

Perhaps I shouldn't say 'it must' because I believe that if something is working, you should keep doing it. I don't want to commit the same error I'm cautioning against by saying, 'You have to do it this way.' But our own research and a large body of literature support this approach: when talking about change, start with the students and an emotionally compelling goal, then figure out how knowledge about effective practices can inform that practice. Of course, the coach must have expertise to share when needed. If the teacher has an emotionally compelling goal and the coach has no strategies to offer to reach the goal, it's not going to be effective. The coach needs to bring knowledge and expertise to the table.

JT: The sentiments about professional and ethical value of teacher autonomy and working in partnership are appreciated. Could you say a bit more about how you see this fitting with developing a school-level approach and degree of consistency in pedagogy (the benefit of consistency being primarily for the students, so they know better what to expect and how to respond)?

JK: When people talk about complexity in educational research, they often use parenting as an example of complex work. Well, if raising two children is complex, think how complex it is to raise 30! Every student is unique, so I'm not overly concerned with the consistency of pedagogy. However, I do believe you can establish boundaries around what you do.

In one of our studies – the one mentioned earlier that had the effect size of 1.02 – we were observing practices. We narrowed our focus to three areas: creating a safe learning environment (classroom management), use of formative assessment, and content planning. So when teachers set their goals, they had to take these areas into consideration, and the coaching followed up accordingly. Observers would check if there was any progress in formative assessment, community building or other practices. The coaches found this focus helpful. That is, you can set limits and boundaries on what you do – having boundaries around the practices you're going to use can be beneficial – but you must still see the teacher as a professional, not as an empty vessel to be filled with ideas.

If something is working, keep doing it. For example, we worked with a school where we initially focused on instructional time, but some teachers didn't have any problems with instructional time, so we shifted our focus. Whatever the area of focus, it must position the teacher as a professional, giving them voice and choice rather than simply telling them what to do.

JT: What's the best way of quality-assuring your coaches and their effectiveness?

JK: In the book *Evaluating Instructional Coaching*, we discuss seven success factors, which are also detailed in *The Definitive Guide to*

Instructional Coaching, along with standards and rubrics that define what effectiveness looks like. We believe that both the coach and the coaching programme should be assessed. It is essential to document your impact, so you need to be able draw a direct line between the coach's actions and the resulting outcomes. This means measuring the goals that have been set and achieved. You can do this in a way that protects the anonymity of your teachers, if that's how your coaching operates. However, you need to be able to say, 'This is what the coach did and these are the outcomes we achieved.'

While *Evaluating Instructional Coaching* is designed to answer the specific questions around evaluating instructional coaching, our website, instructionalcoaching.com, also includes many blog postings and free resources related to the topic.

What concerns me is that sometimes coaches are evaluated by people who don't understand coaching, using tools actually designed for teachers. To be effective, evaluators need to understand coaching and have a methodology with identified standards for what excellence looks like. They should also have a clear assessment process. Ideally, therefore, evaluators should talk to teachers, the coach should self-reflect and the process should involve whoever the coach reports to, perhaps a principal or headteacher. Ultimately, it's important to assess both the programme and the coach.

JT: What steps would you take to implement instructional coaching in a school that hasn't done it before? Where would you start?

JK: First of all, it is important to recognise that this will not happen overnight. To do it well, it will probably take three to four hours per teacher each week. Often I hear people say that scalability is important or that scalability is needed. But it doesn't do much good if we scale up ineffective practices. What matters is real change. When you work with a teacher and have an unmistakable impact on the classroom, it doesn't last for only this year's class – it'll have an impact on every student that teacher will ever teach. That's what you're affecting – that's the goal.

To get started, you need to understand coaching. I think it's important to study a book like *The Definitive Guide to Instructional Coaching* to understand what you're doing. Beyond this book, there is a plethora of free resources online, over 600 free resources for coaches. Second, I recommend going through a coaching cycle, with some rigour, with someone in the school who is highly regarded. Having a person who is excited to be a coach work with an expert teacher is important because if you start with a struggling teacher, it might seem like only those who aren't good teachers get coaches. Instead, start with influential people, so others will think, 'If [a great school teacher/leader] is doing this, maybe I should do it, too.' In short, learn how the process works and do a few cycles to document everything to see what's happening – that's the starting point.

JT: I agree that starting with the children and looking at what's going to help them know more, remember more, and learn better, is important. Where do you stand on bringing consistency and individuality together? Is having a bank of pedagogical techniques that everyone is well trained in and understands important? Should teachers have a toolkit to adapt and meet the needs of their students? Where do consistency and individuality meet?

JK: One of my goals over the next year is to convince Tom Sherrington that this model of instructional coaching is what he should use for WalkThrus. I don't know if it will work; maybe he will end up changing my mind about consistency instead. I'm open to the conversation and have enjoyed every conversation I've had with him. He and Oliver are not just brilliant at what they do; they're also good people.

Honestly, I think consistency is more about power and control. Emphasis on consistency often keeps teachers from being full professionals who use their discretion to do their job. If we strive for consistency, therefore, it is important to ensure that every teacher has a voice in the process and plays a genuine part in it. Otherwise, we treat teachers like unskilled labourers rather than professionals. Professionals use their discretion to do what they need to do.

The evidence overwhelmingly shows that allowing people to have a voice leads to positive change in ways that excluding their input does not. But usually consistency becomes the focus, as opposed to the voice of teachers. If we want the voice of teachers heard when it comes to consistency, the teachers should be involved in deciding what practices work, because they're the ones who work with the children.

Also, if we focus on practices instead of changes in the kids, it will end up creating a lot of work. You will need to constantly remind people to do specific things, which becomes more about pushing than pulling. When you push in coaching, it's like pushing a car up a hill – you push hard, but you don't get there in the end. Pulling in coaching, on the other hand, involves setting emotionally compelling goals that drive the process forward.

Ultimately, what makes a difference is a teacher who is passionate about helping kids working with a coach who is deeply committed to making a difference. When that happens, we will see a palpable, unmistakable difference in terms of achievement and engagement. In my opinion, that's more important than everyone doing the same teaching practices in every classroom.

JT: Are different strategies needed at different times in a school's or teacher's journey? Is the coaching approach as effective for developing talented teachers as it is for ensuring struggling teachers improve rapidly?

JK: I find that struggling teachers are the most sensitive to being told what to do. They need expertise to hit their goals, but the coach can handle this in two ways. They can go to a teacher and say, 'Here are some things you did well and some suggestions for improvement' or they can set a goal with the teacher and ask them what they think they might do differently to achieve it. If the teacher doesn't offer meaningful ideas, the coach can blend their ideas with the teacher's and decide together which ones inspire the most confidence and are most likely to achieve the desired outcome. This approach is respectful; besides, it helps teachers develop independence and problem-solving skills.

At the same time, the coach can still share ideas in the context of the teacher making decisions about what they do, regardless of whether they are a brand-new teacher or an experienced, award-winning one. Often, when approached and asked for suggestions first, the teacher says exactly what the coach would have suggested. Honouring the choice of teachers is both practical and respectful. The coach would be doing a disservice to the teacher if they didn't share their ideas, but they should strive to let the teacher come to conclusions themselves.

JT: Are there any benefits to having coaches who are subject specialists? For example, as a history teacher, should you have a history coach?

JK: In terms of content expertise, in a small sample of instructional coaches, we found that those who worked outside their content area felt they were more effective because they avoided jumping straight to telling the teacher what to do. This may not be generalisable, however. For example, I feel more comfortable coaching inside my subject-specific area of English. But I have heard others say that working with teachers outside their subject area makes them more effective because it allows them to slip into the shoes of the student.

Of course, if a coach's job is curriculum-related (serving more as a curriculum coach than an instructional coach), they absolutely need to be content experts. You can't guide someone through a curriculum you don't understand. So the question is: is the focus on creating a safe learning environment and high-impact teaching practices or is it on curriculum? If it is on curriculum, then you need to have someone with content expertise.

Chapter 11
Leadership 55 wisdom – understanding the finances

Back in the days when he was director-general of the BBC, I heard Greg Dyke say to an assembled audience of senior school leaders: 'Don't leave the money to anyone else, it's too important.' It was one of the greatest pieces of advice I had ever heard. No matter how idealistic new headteachers might be, how determined they are that improving teaching and learning will always be the priority, if they don't have a really good understanding of the money, they will come a cropper. If you want to be a headteacher, ensure you have a great grasp of the budget and someone to manage it for you who knows what they are doing, preferably from a business background.

Things have changed remarkably since I began my first headship. Back in 2003, heads had a great deal of autonomy over school spending. Many modern headteachers have no direct responsibility for spending the school budget. Even if you have to apply to the trust board to buy a box of paperclips, it is essential, as Dyke said, that you understand the budget and the relationship between decisions of spending the budget and students' outcomes.

What I didn't understand when I began as a headteacher was the hugely important relationship between your school budget and the education that you provide for the students who attract that money in the first place. I soon learned. My first taste of headship came with the rather unsavoury task of balancing a budget. Before I was appointed, the governing body had already done their sums and predicted a £300,000 year-end budget deficit. They had made the irrevocable decision that we had to reduce most year groups by one whole teacher's worth of classes. It meant Set 4 and Set 5 being combined in certain subjects in a number of year groups. It was then that I had my first glimpse of the educational impact of financial cuts: behaviour in those combined groups, especially in Year 9, was predictably shocking. It was absolute chaos.

Seven months later, the financial year end saw a £150,000 surplus. The governors had been £450,000 out in their financial predictions. Those classes hadn't needed to be combined. Those students suffered because amateurs were in charge of the finances. I pledged not to let that happen again. I made a promise to learn how to run a multimillion-pound budget.

When it comes to understanding the school budget, nothing quite beats hands-on experience. Good headteachers trust their colleagues to manage budgets. I was lucky to work under Chris Bridge, a headteacher who gave me total responsibility (and accountability) for spending the erstwhile Technology College budget, some £150,000 p.a. It helped me understand finances and was the best preparation I could have had for the moment when I was responsible (along with the governing body) for the whole school budget.

Developing great teachers is your priority. As school budgets tighten across the globe in this age of austerity, you have to resist the urge to squeeze every last hour of teaching out of your teachers; rather, you must give your teachers time and space to work on their practice and target the budget to allow that.

We have to stop guessing about what works. School budgets are getting tighter and tighter; consequently, it is even more important that every penny we have left to spend impacts positively upon improving the quality of teaching and through to student outcomes. So focus on what the evidence says has the best chance of working.

Here are my top five tips for headteachers for understanding the finances:

1. **Find a course that unpicks the relationship between curriculum planning and budget.** There are good ones. Sam Ellis, ASCL's erstwhile expert of all things budgetary, used to run such a programme. He was superb.
2. **Have a funding expert you meet once a week** and brief your trade union reps regularly on budget issues. A finance manager needs to tell you warts and all what is happening with the budget. I have told mine I cannot tolerate budget surprises. Simple things like adding 3% for inflation, and calculating moves up the pay spine, all see your costs rise by significant sums annually. Ask your finance manager to explain all these simple nuances to budget management.
3. **Keep in touch with all the DfE's budget announcements.** You have to work hard at this. It is hugely complicated, especially at the moment. Beware of pay increases that are only funded for one year by a special grant, which you might well have to pick up the tab for in the following year. The DfE seems to ignore the fact that school budgets are impacted by rising costs – all we ever hear about are the so-called increases in funding, not how those increases are reduced in real terms by significant increases in costs. Be vigilant and always budget for the worst-case scenario.
4. **Understand the difference between revenue and capital.** In revenue, the impact of a budget-related decision multiplies down the years, whether you are spending or cutting. If you cut staffing next year by one FTE teacher, that saves you ca. £45,000 next year, and three years on it will have reduced your balance by ca. £135,000. The reverse is true if you plan to have one extra teacher next year. Capital comprises one-off payments that do not, usually, have an impact beyond the year in which the spending takes place. Unless you are in a PFI contract…

5. In the end, **ensure you have enough to pay the wages**. The rest you can get by on, but the wages are the thing. Staffing is your biggest spending commitment. The thing is if high-quality teaching is the key to great student outcomes, then spending money on great staff is a good thing. Without great staff in front of students, aided by a great support staff team, you are going to struggle to provide the high-quality education your students deserve. I have always appointed the best teacher on the day when recruiting – even if there was an almost as good cheaper one available.

And if I was allowed a sixth tip, it would be…treat your school's money as preciously as if it were your own!

Chapter 12
A conversation on assessment with Professor Becky Allen

John Tomsett (JT): In our first Leadership 55 webinar, Becky, we heard Dylan Wiliam talk about assessment. Now you're going to explore the conflict between subject knowledge architecture and how we assess attainment and progress in that subject within the demands of reporting to pupils, parents, headteachers and governors, and the uniformity usually desired at that point. Am I on the right track?

Professor Becky Allen (BA): You are indeed. Thank you very much for inviting me. We're here in 2022, in England. I'm going to make an educated guess that one of your school improvement priorities is related to curriculum. Maybe you are the exceptional school that isn't thinking about this. I talk to many schools and it's quite unusual to meet one where someone isn't doing some hard thinking in this area. I wonder how this thinking is going for you. I wonder if you've reached the part where you feel some discomfort with your assessment system as a consequence of your curriculum thinking. I'd argue if you haven't reached these points of dissonance yet, then perhaps you aren't thinking hard enough about the nature of the challenge. This is the challenge I want to talk to you about today: how can we reconcile talking about attainment in a manner that is faithful to the diversity of subject knowledge architecture and yet accommodates parents', headteachers' and governors' needs for clear and consistent interpretation? I want to begin by discussing why these tensions necessarily exist.

We have variation in curriculum and knowledge architecture across the subjects that we teach in schools. These require radically different assessment approaches. Educators often describe classroom instruction as being based around this three-legged stool of curriculum, assessment and pedagogy. The thing about three-legged stools is that they are exceptionally stable, provided each leg is crafted to sit nicely alongside the others. What does curriculum and knowledge architecture tell us about what our assessment leg needs to look like? Well, it tells us a great deal. Once we know and understand whether we are teaching a subject with very hierarchical knowledge structures or a cumulative subject, it tells us something about how important it is for us to revisit last year's learning in the assessments that we do. It tells us something about how clear and well ordered the schema is likely to be in our subject.

Hierarchical subjects that tend to be well ordered by their nature lend themselves really well to things like short-answer and multiple-response questions, for example. Knowledge architecture tells us whether it's possible in our subject to teach theoretical ideas in the abstract or whether depth of understanding can only ever be revealed through application to context. This matters for us in assessment. It tells us what sorts of prompt materials we necessarily do or don't have to use within assessments. It tells us the extent to which we're able to say something about a student's understanding in the abstract or only ever within a particular context. We need to know how ideas and notions of performance within a subject are related. Performance is what we observe in assessments; it's the only thing we can ever observe. It tells us whether we're trying to assess performance within one construct – being good at something – or within multiple constructs that can sit alongside each other in a subject.

Our goal, and I think the goal of psychometricians, is to measure learning. Whereas for teachers, we don't plan to measure learning as an end in itself. Our goal is always to promote learning within the school. Sometimes we need to measure attainment, but that is because we're serving a bigger purpose within our school, which is to promote learning. Our assessment system should be designed to promote learning.

JT: That was really great. Thank you so much. I think that since KS3 levels went and the inspection framework changed to focus upon curriculum, people are a bit confused. You hear the phrase 'The curriculum is the progression model'. If you've got the curriculum sequenced properly, effectively and logically, then the more you cover of it, the more you're making progress. I think people have been using that phrase 'curriculum is the progression model' and almost been scared of putting their head above the parapet and saying, 'Actually, I don't understand what the hell that means in relation to assessment.' I think people are getting in a right muddle. I don't know what your thoughts are about that.

BA: When you Google that statement now, you will see it on dozens of assessment policies across schools. I think it's an enormously unhelpful statement because it's incomplete. As you say, it doesn't tell you anything about what you should do. That's at best. At worst, it's worse than incomplete; it's actually damaging. The reason why it's damaging is it leads people to think that the way we should do assessment is to do that horrible thing that used to go on, particularly in primary schools, around can-do statements. Let's just write the list of the curriculum and then we're just going to tick them off as people do them. Then we end up in this crazy situation where teachers are having to sit at home entering 1500 data points on whether students can do particular things at some point in time.

It just doesn't begin to represent how complex it is to think about what is the nature of being able to demonstrate you're able to do something in a subject at any particular point in time. Questions of when we learn things, why don't we remember everything? What does it take for us to recall something in a particular type of context? Can we recall it with prompts when we see a multiple-choice question, or is this a piece of information that we're capable of drawing on within an open long-essay question where we're given considerable latitude about how we reconstruct knowledge in order to create answers to questions? To me, it really undermines the complexity of assessment.

To say something about the assessment world that I find frustrating and the thing that's led me to think I should write a book about it is that when you read books on how to do assessments, they don't seem to mention the fact that there are different subjects with different knowledge architectures. You'll read a section on saying ten great things about multiple-choice questions and why you should do them more. Then you can visit schools and they say, 'We told everybody at the end of Year 8 test you should be doing multiple-choice questions.' Then you go and see what the drama department is doing and it's completely insane. You think, well, in a way that's happened because the assessment world doesn't understand that in order to do assessment in schools, we have to be experts in all the other things that teachers are expert in. We can't ask psychometricians to write school assessments. In order to write school assessments, we have to be experts in behavioural psychology and curriculum and pedagogy and really think deeply about the nature of knowledge architecture. Also, we need to think about the agents – the people in schools who are involved in this process – and what their role is in using assessment to promote learning within schools.

JT: Becky, it's been an absolute pleasure. Thank you very much for your insights.

Chapter 13
Leadership 55 wisdom – change management

Understanding change management

I had little idea about how to conduct change when I began my first headship. I made a cataclysm of errors (my choice of collective noun) in the first few years of leading a school. Certainly, the misguided sense that *more is more* was at the heart of my naive approach to enacting change. The thing is, less is more, *always*. I would actually say, *less but better*. School leaders invariably feel safe when we have lots of plans to demonstrate the efforts we are making to improve our schools. In the past I have been horribly guilty of thinking *more is more*!

My first school development plan as a headteacher was a beast, only portable by supermarket trolley. When I presented it to the governing body, the meeting was on the first floor and my PA Rosie and I, with 20 copies of the thing to carry, had to take the lift. It had 38 development initiatives. I wasn't interested in getting *a few essential things right*. I wanted to get everything right straight away.

That governing body meeting where I presented *my* first plan (of course it was *mine* – I had to prove myself as a headteacher and there was no way anyone else was going to tell me what to do) lasted until 11:30pm. Not only did I circulate hard copies of my SDE (school development encyclopaedia), I had 127 PowerPoint slides (of largely text copied verbatim from the SDE itself) to help me tell governors what we were going to do over the next year.

It was great. I loved it. I gained some odd satisfaction from the strain and pain of giving birth to the thing, the weekends spent typing the beast up while my wife and kids entertained themselves, an absent father in the next room. And I had no idea how I was going to measure whether what I had planned had worked.

Looking back now, it's embarrassing to think of that first development plan. But the culture of fear breeds backside-covering among early career headteachers. It's really easy to implement extensive interventions in an attempt to raise headline results figures just so that you can point to how much you did to improve results when the results turn out to be disappointing in August. *I know the results are rubbish, but we worked really hard – look at all the things we did...*

And then there is the difficult challenge of realising just a single specific change. What I did not understand is just how difficult it is to enact what seemed to be even the simplest alteration to practice within a school. Teachers and schools are conservative places. Change is rarely greeted with enthusiasm. And if you have 112 teachers and 70 support staff in a school, like we did at Huntington, ensuring that a change to practice is implemented with 100% fidelity is a huge challenge.

So, if you are a headteacher and are preparing to implement changes to the school you lead, here are my top five tips for *understanding the change process*:

1. **Know where you are on the sigmoid curve.** Whenever an organisation implements change there is a general pattern of

development explained by sigmoid curve analysis, shown in this first diagram:

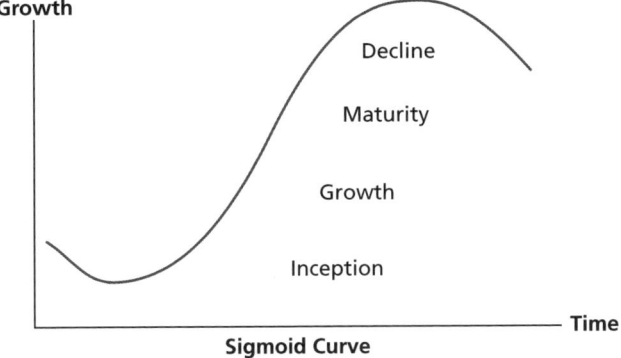
Sigmoid Curve

The key issue is when to introduce the next phase of change, explored in the second diagram:

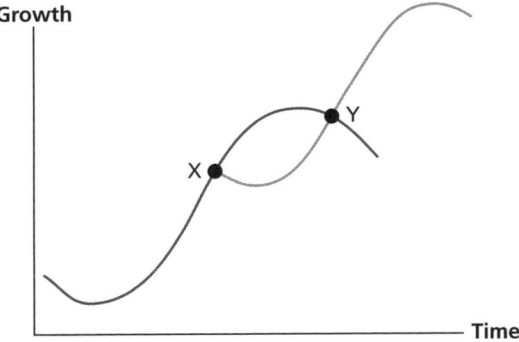

You want to reach point Y on an upward, not downward, trajectory, but when can you tell that it's time to jump off the first curve? Riding the first curve while cultivating the second is always the best option; clinging to the first and trying to prolong it is a pointless waste of energy. When all is well and you are at the top of your game, then it's probably the time to plan your next curve.

I once asked our SLT where they think Huntington is on its sigmoid curve. The numbers indicate how many of us thought we were at those specific points on the curve.

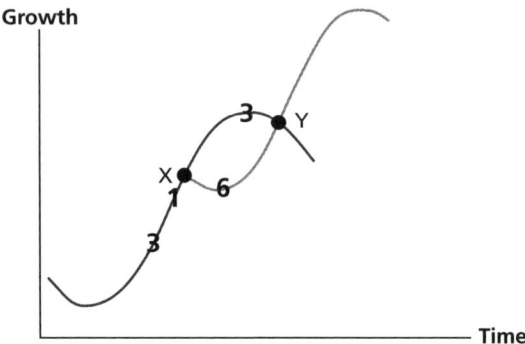

2. **Get a few essential things right.** Sir Tim Brighouse's *The jigsaw of a successful school* is sharp stuff and required reading for all early career headteachers. It embodies the principle of keeping things coherently simple. In his introduction, he makes the following observation about change and school improvement:

> ...whenever I've visited a school, which has recovered its sense of direction and pride after falling on hard times [...] I ask the (usually new) head teacher, "Well, what did you do?" The reply is always the same. Whatever the head teacher's style, whether understated and calm, cool and determined or outrageously busy, the reply usually contains the phrase: "Well it's not rocket science. We just concentrated on getting a few essential things right".

'[...] getting a few essential things right'. Just let that phrase sink in.

It depends where you are in the development cycle of a school, but wherever you find yourself on the development cycle, pare down your change priorities and do a small number of things really well. Easier to say than do, perhaps, but school improvement is not hard, as long as you keep it simple and focused on what matters.

3. **Learn about the change process.** One book that helped which I read before I began was *Leading in a Culture of Change* by Michael Fullan.[3] Another publication from the Canadian leadership guru, *The Six Secrets of Change*, I have found hugely useful. My leadership of change at two schools has taught me many things, most of which Fullan articulates in his book *Leading in a Culture of Change*. His

---

3 Fullan, M. (2001) *Leading in a Culture of Change*. San Francisco, CA: Jossey Bass.

six secrets are not secrets any more – since he's published them – and I'm not sure they ever were; I think they are common sense:

1. The goal is not to innovate the most.
2. It is not enough to have the best ideas.
3. Appreciate the implementation dip.
4. Redefine resistance.
5. Reculturing is the name of the game.
6. Never a checklist, always complexity.

So much of what Fullan says here I discovered the hard way, through first-hand experience; perhaps one has to live through professional strife before one can accept that Fullan-style wisdom is true.

4. **Look to the commercial world.** I have never desired to be a businessman, but I do, however, learn from business practices. A few years ago, I adopted what's called 'blue ocean strategy' in order to have a structure for implementing change. We spend more time now thinking about how we implement change than what that change might be. Implementation is woven into our planning, not an afterthought. It works brilliantly and has helped us improve teaching and learning no end.

5. **Keep learning about implementing change.** Most recently Professor Jonathan Sharples co-authored an EEF guidance report on how to plan the implementation of your interventions entitled *Putting Evidence to Work – A School's Guide to Implementation*.[4] It is essential reading for all school leaders, and I don't say that lightly. It is a game-changer, as far as I am concerned. It introduced me to the concept of implementation activities; that is, activities that you detail in your plannin, which help ensure that the enacted change is as faithful as possible to the change you planned. The idea is outlined here in a series of slides, where we identify the issue – in this case, a curriculum issue – then go to the desired outcome, then detail the change required, then identify the implementation

---

4 Sharples, J., Eaton, J. and Boughelaf, J. (2024) *Putting Evidence to Work – A School's Guide to Implementation*. London: Education Endowment Foundation. Available at: https://educationendowmentfoundation.org.uk/education-evidence/guidance-reports/implementation (Accessed: 30 April 2025).

activities in all their prosaic dullness, and then finally envisage the outcomes of the implementation activities. I promise you it works.

Curriculum issue	The Year 7 English curriculum is not meeting the needs of our highest starting students and is not developing all students' foundational knowledge.
Student outcomes	Year 7 students of all starting points will know: the narrative of 'Robinson Crusoe', its socioeconomic context, its place as the 'first English novel', etc.
Change required	We are going to swap the current novel 'Holes' for 'Robinson Crusoe' from September 2019.
Implementation activities	Jane to have 2 days off TT to shape materials for teaching 'Robinson Crusoe' to mixed attainment classes and Jim will co-write the SoL on day 3.
Implementation outcomes	A scheme of learning that is pitched high, has a low floor, is challenging for all, and is well-resourced and easily accessible on the departmental e-folder.

In January 2018 we used this approach to implement seven months of preparatory work on improving the progress of our most vulnerable learners. Eighteen months later, for the first time, our disadvantaged Year 11 students had a positive overall P8 score and their P8 score for EBacc subjects was +0.22. Still not as good as we wanted, but in a school where 92% of our students are from a white British background, it was a respectable outcome.

And if I was allowed a sixth tip: before you implement, carry out a pre-mortem. I always anticipate what might go wrong. It's safer that way, and I can only be pleasantly surprised when my pessimistic anticipations do not materialise.

At Huntington we have formalised such pessimistic thinking within the implementation of all important strategic developments we undertake. After we have completed our blue ocean strategy analysis and identified our implementation activities, we undertake a pre-mortem. Instead of working out what caused a development to fail *after* it has failed as we would in a post-mortem, we assume it has already failed *before* we have begun and try to predict what would cause such failure. Once we have established what might cause our developments to run aground, we agree a list of actions to prevent such an eventuality.

Our pre-mortem idea was derived from an article by psychologist Gary Klein.[5] He cites research by Mitchell, Russo and Pennington, which found 'that *prospective hindsight* – imagining that an event has already occurred – increases the ability to correctly identify reasons for future outcomes by 30%'.[6] Klein devised his pre-mortem, the distinctive feature of which is the assumption by the team that the development has completely failed.

Psychologically, this assumption of total failure allows members of the team to speak more frankly than if they were merely thinking about why the development in question might not work. This sense of what *has* happened instead of what *could* happen helps the team visualise the assumed failure with greater clarity. The team gains a similar lucidity when hypothesising about why the failure *happened*.

We used the pre-mortem technique when implementing our new pastoral structure. Our write-up of our discussions began: 'It's July 2016 and the Pastoral Review has failed to deliver on any of its objectives.' We created a table on one side of A4 which had three headings:

Reason for failure	How it could have been avoided	Person responsible for prevention

Once established, the pre-mortem becomes a regular agenda item at the team's implementation meetings.

---

5 Klein, G. (2007) 'Performing a Project Premortem', *Harvard Business Review*, September. Available at https://hbr.org/2007/09/performing-a-project-premortem (Accessed: 30 April 2025).
6 Mitchell, D. J., Russo, J. E. and Pennington, N. (1989) 'Back to the future: Temporal perspective in the explanation of events', *Journal of Behavioural Decision Making*, 2(1), pp. 25–38.

Chapter 14
A conversation on Ofsted with Malcolm Willis

Malcolm Willis: Ofsted top ten tips for school leaders

Leadership 55 is very specific and focused. It reminded me of the paper that ASCL released last year about Ofsted, which many of you have probably read. They make wise comments about the nature of an Ofsted inspection and how it reduces a complex organisation like a school to just one of four judgements. This afternoon, I will be even more reductionist by breaking down Ofsted into just ten areas or things to consider. I want it to be short, sharp, focused and specific.

So, coming from the perspective of an Ofsted inspection, I was thinking:
1. If I were a headteacher, what would I want to consider before Ofsted arrived?
2. What are some things that schools sometimes don't do well during inspections?
3. What are the inspection questions and probes that sometimes catch schools out?

For this chapter, I have tried to identify those key points that I hope are useful and practical. Some will be obvious because we're familiar with the Ofsted framework. Schools know it well and have done extensive work on their curriculum and its implementation. But nonetheless, here are ten areas to consider before Ofsted arrives.

The phone call

Firstly, prepare for the phone call. If you haven't done a preparatory phone call with HEP, I suggest you book one because they can be very helpful in thinking about and articulating your school. A good lead inspector will give you an opportunity in that phone call to provide a narrative about your school. This is a key opportunity to describe your school, show how well you understand its community and the learning needs of your students, and how you've matched the curriculum to them. Consider too its areas of strength and where it still requires development. From September, the phone call will reflect Ofsted not undertaking deep dives if you have an ungraded inspection.

Think about the phone call and plan it out on paper. Talk to your leadership team about their roles and responsibilities for that phone call. Ensure you have the details of previous inspections, areas for improvement, the actions you've taken and their impact.

Be clear about presenting the relative strengths of your school, particularly in the subject areas, because Ofsted will ask about those during the deep dives. You will likely have specific thoughts about the areas you prefer to be explored or avoided. How you articulate the strengths and relative weaknesses of those areas is crucial. Be prepared to articulate the particular strengths and areas for further development at the school.

Consider carefully the language you use and how it will be interpreted. Practise and get it well organised; this can get the inspection off to a good start and establish a positive relationship with the lead inspector.

Safeguarding

If I were a headteacher, one of the first and most important things I would always focus on is safeguarding. It seems obvious, and we sometimes address it last, but it's critical. You know from the framework that Ofsted focus in on: identify, help and manage. They evaluate how well the school identifies issues and concerns, helps young people and manages the process, including recruiting staff suitable to work with children.

Audit and check your single central record. Audit, check and probe into your system. Do you have unresolved cases or cases that have been referred but are still pending? What does the time gap look like between initial concerns and referrals? Are individual case notes thorough and up to date? Have a few key case histories prepared, including, for example, an LAC (looked after child). Make sure you thoroughly probe your safeguarding system and ensure that everybody is clear on their roles, responsibilities and actions to take if they have a concern.

The DSL (designated safeguarding lead) should be aware of how Ofsted inspections of the local authority's children's services have informed safeguarding practices within the school. Therefore, if they haven't looked at the Ofsted inspection of the local authority's children's services, it's a good idea to do so and consider its relevance to the school.

It's also good to show that you are engaged in a cycle of continuous improvement. For example, you may be asked: what are your next steps to improve safeguarding practice, and how has this been informed by your Section 175 audit?

Some DSLs may not be familiar with the term, but the 2002 Education Act set up Section 175, which is a statutory duty for schools' governing bodies to carry out an annual review of the school's policies and procedures and audit their safeguarding. The Section 175 audit is useful for using that detailed review to create an action plan around the needs of your particular setting.

One always wants to know how well the school understands its own children and the specific safeguarding issues for them and their community. It is good if this information then feeds into the personal development programme. The PSHE programme should have some flexibility and can be re-sequenced according to safeguarding needs, creating a helpful feedback loop.

It is also important to ask what your pupils tell you about sexual harassment, and what have you done as a result? Schools are more aware of this now and it remains very important. If alternative provision is used, probe the solidity of the safeguarding information around it. Don't just stop there, either – understand how well your school knows the achievement and wellbeing of the young people placed in alternative provision. Just because they are in alternative provision doesn't mean they're not the school's responsibility. This can sometimes be an area of weakness.

Quality of education

Number three is the quality of education. It's self-evident that this would be here. In my experience, intent is increasingly well planned. Schools have had time to think about the curriculum and are aware of the need to structure, plan and sequence it. Many middle leaders can now articulate it extremely well. However, a middle leader's articulation may not be reflected in the implementation of the curriculum in the classroom. That is the most important place – the classroom – and inspectors always have critical questions on pedagogy and how well all pupils are learning, including those with SEND.

Ofsted does not judge individual lessons or have a preferred teaching style, but they do probe how well pupils are learning, using their definition: 'knowing more and remembering more'. Last year, the focus homed in on SEND, particularly on how the curriculum is adapted. We could have a whole session on curriculum adaptation, but it's worth highlighting that the word 'differentiation' is now discouraged. However, I think there are some strategies within differentiation that are similar to those in adaptation.

Essentially, good adaptation involves teachers knowing their pupils well. Assessment is a key part of this. Good assessment leads to good teaching because if you know what your pupils do and don't know, you know what to teach next. Your sequencing and assessment for teaching come logically from formative and summative assessments. Checking for misunderstandings and knowing what to teach next are fundamental to excellent teaching.

I often hear teachers talk about having a challenging curriculum, but challenge should not be simply about making things harder. It should be about understanding what a child knows, the complexity of their knowledge, how it interrelates and how to build upon it. Appropriate curriculum planning and sequencing are crucial to support learning, and knowing what the child knows and doesn't know is essential for planning the next steps.

Returning to SEND, inspectors will occasionally ask for an EHCP (translated into information for teachers, such as a pupil profile) and then visit the class, talk to the pupil and discuss with the teacher how they address the pupil's needs. This is not explicitly in the EIF, but it is something some inspectors do. The key thing is how well staff know their pupils and their needs, and how well the pupils can articulate what they know and have remembered.

Reading

My fourth point is reading. For some secondary schools, this is an area that may need further development. Many have made significant progress in the last two years or so, but there is still work to be done. If you're a secondary lead for reading, learning from primary practice can be very beneficial; look at how Ofsted inspects primary reading. You may have seen online that Ofsted 'help sheets' have been released, including one on primary reading. There are excellent elements in it that apply to secondary schools, such as developing a love of reading across the whole school.

How do you go about that? You would expect a range of strategies in place to do that. Also consider how you identify children who need to catch up with their peers. How are they helped to do so? An area of weakness I often see in secondary schools is not just identifying pupils and putting interventions in place but evaluating the effectiveness of those interventions and following up. Reading is a crucial area and will be looked at in the quality of education.

Key people

My fifth point is about key people. Sometimes we can forget that in addition to middle leaders, there are other critical individuals who make significant contributions to the inspection process. It's important to spend time preparing them.

First, the receptionist. They are critical because they are the first people that Ofsted meet. Ensure all their safeguarding practices are correct and they know how to welcome Ofsted into your school. This sounds obvious, but they aren't always as well prepared as they might be.

Secondly, the SENDCO. In an ungraded inspection, not all SENDCOs are spoken to, but they have a critical role and are often interviewed. Their clarity on how they enable children with SEND to be identified, the quality of their provision mapping and how they evaluate children's progress are all key factors in their response.

Inspectors also usually meet with the lead for attendance and behaviour. Behaviour is one of the spotlight areas in ungraded inspections. Additionally, they usually meet with the lead for careers education, information, advice and guidance (CEIAG) because it's important to know about that wider development. Short meetings with personal development leaders can help focus on what they're doing to drive this forward in the school.

Governor preparation is critical; they need to be clear on their three areas of responsibility and statutory elements. If asked about the Equalities Act and how the school meets its requirements, ensure that they are prepared for such a question. If you're uncertain, check that the equality objectives on your website are updated as needed and ensure there's an access policy in place. More broadly and arguably more importantly, consider equality in the creation of all policies and practices throughout the school.

Staff wellbeing and workload

Number six is a spotlight area in an ungraded inspection, and it is to be prepared for questions on staff wellbeing and workload. What's your evidence for that? It could be in the form of surveys and focus groups and it's good to show that you have listened to staff. What do they tell you? Does it differ from the surveys? Do responses vary at different times? What are their pressure points? How are you responding to that? How do you support them, especially at the end of what's been a difficult time nationally and in schools in particular? Schools are pressured places at the best of times, so what do you do for that?

And what do you do as a head if there is some negative staff feedback? Be prepared for how you might respond to such a scenario.

The Baker clause

My seventh – I'm sure secondary schools are aware of this – is how you meet the requirements of the Baker clause, which has recently been strengthened. The Baker clause requires schools to give their pupils access to information about technical education providers. This has not been very well done by some schools in all parts of the country. Now, there are some new and specific expectations, so if you're not aware of those, look them up and make sure your school complies. There is a phrase in the Baker clause that is required for the report during graded inspections. It does not go into the report during ungraded inspections, but you should expect an inspector to enquire about that.

Gaming and off-rolling

Number eight involves gaming and off-rolling, which are spotlight areas in ungraded inspections. This is perhaps less of a national issue than it was around 2018, when there was concern about schools moving pupils illegally off roll and schools trying to manipulate their data. However, don't be surprised if inspectors have looked at examination entry patterns and challenge you on why some subjects are entered in a manner that might not benefit pupils. For example, if you have all pupils doing particular subjects, be prepared to explain why it benefits all.

Website

My ninth tip is to check your website if you haven't already done so. It is one of the first contacts that the lead inspector has with your school. Surprisingly there are often gaps, even when you would expect people to have checked it. Sometimes not all the safeguarding policies are present. There is usually a child protection policy, but things like whistleblowing policies might be missing. You should have a complete suite of policies, so check that those are there.

Surprisingly often policy documents have expired beyond their review dates. It might seem like a minor issue, and it doesn't entirely upset the inspection, but it looks careless. You don't want lead inspectors to think your school is disorganised. Good management, running a school well, ensuring the organisation works efficiently and that systems and processes deliver effectively are part of what makes a good school. So, sweat the small stuff – check the dates and so on.

Sometimes SEND information is not present or is of low quality. If you want your SEND information report looked at, have an organisation like HEP look at that for you. A good information report, with a Q&A element, that informs parents about the school's provision is important. Also make sure that the report is accessible; it tells you about the school's inclusivity and approach to children with special educational needs.

Finally, check that the governor information is up to date and conforms to expectations. Governor information on websites tends to vary, so ensure you comply with the requirements.

Manage the inspection

Manage the inspection through good preparation and a process of continuous improvement that focuses on securing on the maintenance of a school with safe, happy children and staff and a good curriculum taught well.

Questions

John Tomsett (JT): If a school is currently 'outstanding', how can they articulate what their weak areas are without saying explicitly that anything is weak?

Malcolm Willis (MW): That's such a good question. I think it revolves around the language you use, emphasising the desire to further develop the excellence of an area. You can't articulate it as weak or use pejorative language. At the same time, I would hope that any lead inspector would understand that within a complex organisation like a school, different areas need attention at different times to remain cutting-edge and retain their excellence. So, it is very much about how you frame it. However, be clear on how you use high-quality self-evaluation to ensure continuous improvement.

JT: When it comes to wellbeing, staff often comment about the stress of Ofsted, the never-ending pressure and the seemingly impossible immaculate standards required for 'outstanding'. How can school leaders deal with that?

MW: Always focus on excellent teaching, ensuring that pupils are happy at your school, and supporting and working with your staff. It's about the quality of leadership and your openness. Ultimately, if you get the classrooms, teaching and climate right, then Ofsted should take care of itself.

Chapter 15
Leadership 55 wisdom – coping with the loneliness

I had been exercised, early in my first headship, by a lad from the town who was known to dabble in drugs. He would loiter at the stile at the end of the school day, mixing with some of our most vulnerable students. One darkening November afternoon in my first term, I confronted him boldly, accusing him of being a drug dealer and directing him, in no uncertain terms, to stay away from my students. He stood his ground. He wasn't, by a matter of inches, on school property. And he had an audience of some of my most challenging charges.

As I walked away, back down the path into school, the sense of loneliness was palpable. He stood there, victorious. I could hear the laughter and the jeers. Things got worse when his parents complained to the governing body. I literally sunk to the floor in my office when that news came through, in complete despair. I had mucked up. A week later I faced his mum and dad in my office where I had to apologise to them for making unsubstantiated accusations about their son. I felt humiliated. Kevin, our older, hugely experienced, burly assistant headteacher, reassured me. He frequented the local pubs. He knew the town. He was sure nothing would really come of it. In a week's time it would be old news. And, of course, he was right.

Later that first year I made a terrifically difficult decision about an internal appointment. Two strong candidates for a senior post and I decided to appoint neither. That was tough. For what seemed an eternity, every time I walked into the staffroom colleagues stopped talking. I thought about that issue day and night and all weekend. I went fishing with my mate Nick and it was all I could contemplate. Even when I caught a pike, I was wondering about how to sort the mess out at school. Nick knew something was wrong. He chatted it through with me. He was wise about it all. Of course, it would resolve itself. I just had to be patient. Like Kevin before him, he was spot on.

The loneliest moment of my career came in 2010, when our results dipped badly. On that damp August results Wednesday, I sat in my car as the rain pummelled down on the roof and wept and wept; I felt like the loneliest man on the entire planet. I finally rang my wife, Louise, who said to me, 'John, come home. We all love you. You can pack it in. It's really not worth it.' Her words were the balm I needed just at that moment. I was very close to quitting. Thanks to Louise, I didn't.

The loneliness of the job comes, in the end, from a mixture of forces: the fact that the buck stops with you; having to have difficult conversations with other adults; the confidentiality of so much of what you have to deal with; the range and number of different people and organisations to whom you are accountable; the sheer vulnerability of the position and how you are more sackable than any other person in your school. So, if you are a headteacher and you are sitting in front of a screen on a Sunday morning feeling distant from your family and worried about next week – if you are feeling just plain *lonely* – here are my top five tips for headteachers for *coping with the loneliness*:

1. **Find someone you can talk to.** The thread through my loneliness examples above is clear. All headteachers need someone they trust with whom they can share their insecurities. In January 2016 the

BBC screened a programme entitled *The Age of Loneliness*. In a poignant documentary, which is affecting yet never mawkish, Sue Bourne interviews a range of people who talk about living in relative solitude. Loneliness, according to Bourne, is 'the silent epidemic'. Bourne's fundamental conclusion is that 'People of all ages missed someone to do nothing with. To chat idly. To sit next to.' And that's it, isn't it? We all need, to a greater or lesser extent, someone with whom to share our lives. And why should headteachers be any different? If there is no one at home to talk to, a good employer will provide you with an experienced leadership coach. Bottling up stuff will only increase the sense of loneliness.

2. **Choose to be a stoic and control how you react to things.** Shakespeare's 'There is nothing either good or bad but thinking makes it so' is rooted in stoic philosophy. Accept that you can control how you react to life's vagaries. You can choose how you think, and knowing this has helped keep me sane. It is worth reflecting upon the fact that here, now, as you read this and take a moment to look back on your life, all the things that have traumatised you, all the disasters that have befallen you, you have survived. Nothing has been as bad as it might have been. Nothing is ever that bad. As the reassuring aphorism goes: 'It will be alright in the end and if it isn't alright, you haven't reached the end yet.' We can surely choose how we react to life's vagaries. All events are neutral; how we interpret them determines whether they are good or bad and how we allow them to affect us. Imagine this… impossible as it might seem, *everything* that happens to you could be good if you chose to think that way.

3. **Learn to compartmentalise.** I have always argued that the work–life balance is a false dichotomy. I enjoyed my job; I was proud to be a head-teacher; my work has always been a central part of my life. For a long time, I have preferred the *work–home* balance, which, combined, constitute my life. But now, much nearer the end of my career than the beginning, I am not sure that I wholly subscribe to my nuanced definition. I heard Cat Scutt speak once at researchED Durham and some research she pointed to made me think. A paper by Klusmann et al. on teacher wellbeing found that some of the most effective teachers maintained a 'healthy detachment' about

their job and 'conserved their personal resources'. What Cat said resonated with me and reminded me of Philip Gould. In his final interview before he died at the age of 61, Gould, Tony Blair's close adviser, said this to Andrew Marr and I have had it pinned on my office wall ever since: 'What would have been better for me would have been to have said, "I'll do what I can do, which I do quite well" and then just push it back a little bit.' Gould's insight came too late for him, but it isn't too late for me or any headteacher. It. Is. Only. A. Job.

4. **Do stuff just for you.** I have a list of things I do that grow my capacity to cope with whatever life throws at me:

- prioritise my family
- reading
- writing
- fishing
- golf
- exercise
- breathing exercises
- recondition old fishing rods.

5. **My most important tip for coping with the loneliness is an eternal truth.** As Francis Bacon knew so well: the best antidote to loneliness is love. *It is the only thing that really matters.* 'But little do men perceive what solitude is, and how far it extendeth. For a crowd is not company; and faces are but a gallery of pictures; and talk but a tinkling cymbal, where there is no love.'

Chapter 16
A conversation on cognitive science with Jade Pearce

Five principles of cognitive science in the classroom

I'm here to talk to you today about five principles from cognitive science. It's not all my wisdom or work in any way. It is from this book, *The researchED Guide to Cognitive Science*, in which I have written one chapter. But there are brilliant contributions from other authors like Adam Boxer, Jonathan Firth, Sarah Cottingham and Lekha Sharma, and the whole book is edited by Kate Jones. The series is edited by Tom Bennett.

What I've tried to do here is pick out five chapters from the book and to give you a flavour of what's included. It's really meant to be a bit of an overview and introduction to cognitive science. Hopefully there will be some nuggets there that you think will be interesting to go have a look at in more depth.

There are five principles that I'm going to have a look at and that come from the first five chapters of the book. So, first of all, we're going to look at cognitive load theory and how we can manage cognitive load for our learners. Then we're going to look at prior knowledge and its impact on learning. That's Sarah Cottingham's chapter, all about meaningful learning and the importance of prior knowledge. Then we're going to have a look at dual coding. Principle four is about interleaving being more effective than blocking. And, finally, we're going to look at spaced retrieval practice and its role in preventing forgetting.

Before all of that, I wanted to just do a very quick overview of the cognitive science model of memory. If you've ever heard me present, you've probably heard me explain this before, but it is the bedrock – the building blocks – and the reason why all of the strategies that we're discussing today are effective.

The cognitive science model of memory is a model for how our memories work. Essentially, it splits our memory into our working memory and our long-term memory. Our working memory is where we consciously think – where we process new content. Our long-term memory is the store of everything we know, have experienced, can do, etc. And essentially, that's learning: when we take something that we're thinking about in our working memory and we encode it into our long-term memory so that we remember it and can retrieve it in the future. Then we can say that we've learned that content, knowledge or skill.

However, we know two things from cognitive science: first of all, we know the capacity of our working memory is limited. Most people can only think of a few chunks of new information, especially complex information, at any one time. If we overload that working memory – like by making our students think about too many new pieces of information at once – it will result in forgetting. They won't be able to hold all of that information in their mind at one time and they'll forget some of it.

So that's the first problem we try to overcome with strategies from cognitive science. The second is that even if we've worked hard to make sure our pupils' working memory isn't overloaded, managed to get them to encode the information we want and they've put it into their long-term memory, unfortunately this may not stay in the long-term memory over time.

You'll all remember things that you studied at school or even at university that, at one point, you knew really well, and now you can hardly remember it. That is because even if something is in our long-term memory, we can forget it unless it is regularly retrieved and put back into our working memory. If we think about it, we remember it. Essentially, that's the model of working memory and it underpins all the principles we're going to look at.

Principle 1: managing cognitive load

Cognitive load is the amount of processing required by the working memory during learning. Depending on how much information we are asking pupils to process and how complex that information is, that will place a load on their working memory (remember, our working memory is limited in how much it can actually handle at one time).

There are two types of cognitive load. The first is intrinsic cognitive load that comes from the content – how complex it is and how much of it there is. This is necessary for learning: when we think about the content and we process it, that is what transfers the knowledge or skill from our working memory to our long-term memory. So that intrinsic load is necessary for learning.

Then we have extraneous cognitive load. This comes from our teaching – how the information, for example, is presented to learners – and it is not productive for learning. There are many things that cause extraneous cognitive load to pupils without improving learning. When we manage cognitive load, we therefore want to reduce the extraneous cognitive load so that the working memory isn't overloaded. Then, we can use the working memory to instead process that intrinsic cognitive load by looking at challenging content and tasks, for example. Cognitive load theory is helpful because it gives us strategies to manage cognitive load, which are called 'effects'. Now we're going to have a look at some of what I think are the main effects we can implement into our teaching.

First of all, we've got the 'worked example effect'. This applies to novice learners and it states that when we are first learning something, studying worked examples is more effective than solving problems. By worked examples, we essentially mean models, but not just models that show an example of a completed task. The model must have more specific instructions. For example, if a teacher were teaching long division, they would provide an example of the first step of solving this problem. With this, they would provide a written explanation of what is actually being done and why. The reason that these examples are more effective is because they make it really clear to pupils how to complete the tasks you want them to complete. They don't have to hold that information, or those steps, in their working memory. They can refer to that worked example and just think about the question that they will then try to solve themselves.

The second effect we can look at is the 'redundancy effect', which essentially says we need to remove redundant information. If we know that our limited working memory can only hold maybe four or five chunks of information, we want to make sure that those four or five chunks we're choosing are the most crucial ones. This means we don't want to give long-winded explanations that include lots of information that our students don't really need to know. We don't want to include instructions that have got six or seven steps when we could have said those instructions in two or three chunks. We don't want presentations or worksheets with lots of redundant information – we want everything to be clear and concise so that our working memory is only taken up with the most important information.

Next is the 'split-attention effect'. Split attention is when you ask pupils to split their attention between two sources. The most common example is when we ask them to look at a diagram and then we have a separate text explanation or key that explains the diagram. Pupils have to split their attention between the diagram and the text, and then mentally integrate them, which takes up space in the working memory. If the two were integrated to begin with, it would result in less cognitive load. We want to ensure that our pupils' attention is not split.

There are several other effects, but the last one we'll discuss for now is the 'expertise reversal effect'. It is really important to realise that the effects we have discussed are only effective when we're initially learning new content or a new skill. When we are first learning something, we want to remove redundant information, we want to integrate our diagrams, we want to provide worked examples, but actually the 'expertise reversal effect' says that as you become more expert in a topic, the things we do to help prevent cognitive overload aren't needed anymore. This means we can remove scaffolding, we can remove guidance, we can stop providing worked examples, etc. over time.

Principle 2: prior knowledge determines learning

The second principle concerns the importance of prior knowledge to our learning, or the relationship between what our pupils know and what they can learn in the future. This is all about schema consolidation. Schema is how knowledge is organised in our long-term memories as webs of interconnected pieces of knowledge. Cognitive science suggests that learning is increased if we can take a new idea and hook it onto something we already know, by consolidating that schema that we already have. In other words, learning is increased if students strongly relate a new idea to what they already know. As teachers, we can take advantage of that in different ways. We can activate pupils' prior knowledge by, for example, doing retrieval practice on what they already know about a topic before we introduce some new content about that topic. Alternatively, we might re-explain something if we don't think pupils are going to have that information in their long-term memories.

We want to make sure that our explanations explicitly link to prior knowledge. That doesn't mean simply referencing that pupils learned something in Year 5 and now they're learning this in Year 6 so they are linked. It means explicitly explaining, 'This is what we learned before. And *this* is how it explicitly links to what we've learned today.' We want to get pupils to do that as well. We want to set tasks for our pupils that require them to explicitly link to their prior knowledge.

To give you an example, if a class is learning about plants in Year 3 and looking back to the learning about plants in Year 1, the teacher might ask pupils to activate their prior knowledge by doing some general practice on what they learned in Year 1 with a little quiz. Then the teacher should explicitly link the two, potentially by saying: 'Okay, in Year 1, you learned about the parts of the plant like the roots, the stem and the leaves. In Year 3, we're going to build on that by looking at how each part of the plant helps it to be healthy. For example, in Year 1, you learned that this is the stem. And now in Year 3, we're learning that the stem carries the water from the roots to the rest of the plant.' Making those links really explicit and clear helps consolidate pupils' schema about plants. To further enhance the learning, a teacher might then ask pupils to link prior knowledge themselves through additional tasks, like the one below.

Tasks linking to prior knowledge: example

- What do plants need to be healthy?
- Label the main parts of the plant on the diagram.
- Why are petals bright in colour?
- What is the function of the stem?
- What are the two functions of the roots?

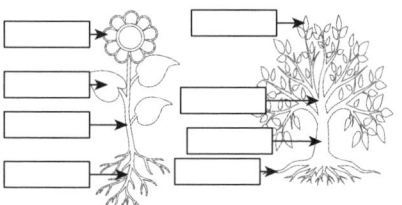

Principle 3: dual coding benefits learning

Principle 3 is about dual coding and how beneficial it is to learning. Essentially, dual coding is combining words and diagrams. It uses the two channels of the working memory – one that can absorb information from spoken or written language and the other that can absorb information from images. If we can represent information using both of those channels, we increase the amount of information that the working memory can process at one time. That means if we use dual coding, combining verbal explanations and diagrams, our pupils can actually think about and process more information in one go.

Again, we want to make sure that while we are using diagrams, we're doing it in a way that benefits learning. So, we want to integrate those diagrams to manage cognitive load and not split attention. We want to continue to remove redundant information from our diagrams. And we want to manage and direct attention – drawing pupils' attention to the most important part of the diagram, or only having one part of the diagram displayed while you're talking about it, and then moving on to the next part of the diagram when your focus turns there. This is preferable to having everything available to pupils all at once.

We might use a diagram if we were learning about the water cycle or a timeline if we were learning about events in history. We might use a Venn diagram if we look at similarities and differences between two concepts. And a T-chart can be used to compare pros and cons.

Drawing is not my strong point, and Adam Boxer, who wrote the chapter on dual coding, included really great examples in it. He also has really great resources on dual coding for teachers that struggle to draw. But hopefully you've got the gist of how beneficial representing information graphically can be.

Principle 4: interleaving is more effective than blocking

The chapter on interleaving in *The researchED Guide to Cognitive Science* was written by Jonathan Firth. Interleaving is the mixing-up of learning material with other material that is slightly different, within one study session. To clarify a misconception here, in the past, interleaving was thought to mean perhaps teaching an hour of history, then an hour of geography and then an hour of science. We now know that is not interleaving. In fact, interleaving occurs only when we mix up similar material and when we do it within a very small timeframe. That contrasts with blocking, which is where you look at all of one type of content and then all of another and so on.

I'll give you some examples to clarify what I mean. Let's say we were categorising species of animals and we wanted to look at whether a certain species is an insect or an arachnid. If we did blocking, we would look at lots of examples of insects and then at lots of examples of arachnids. If we were doing interleaving, we would intersperse examples of an insect, then an arachnid, then an insect, etc. The theory that supports this is called the 'discriminative-contrast hypothesis'. It states that if we interleave and mix examples up, it helps pupils recognise subtle differences between the subject matter and therefore be able to categorise correctly.

The same would occur if we were looking at the differences between metaphors, similes or analogies. With blocking, we would learn all about metaphors and do some practice there, then we would do similes and finally we would do analogies. In interleaving, we would mix those things up: we might look at a metaphor, then a simile and then an analogy, and that actually helps pupils to be able to recognise the differences between them and not confuse them.

The improved learning that occurs through interleaving rather than blocking has been proven again and again by paper after paper, so it is really strongly evidence-informed practice, especially in maths learning, actually, because of that discriminative-contrast hypothesis. What Jonathan does in the book is to look at how we can make interleaving more effective. He says we need to look at similar concepts with subtle differences – not things that are wildly different to one another, but concepts that pupils tend to confuse.

While interleaving, we want to use a small number of examples or concepts and small or brief concepts. You wouldn't want to contrast something like *Romeo and Juliet* with another play – that's too huge. You would need to interleave something within that, that you could do in one lesson or study session.

Interestingly, if you're dealing with really complex material, you might start interleaving *after* block practice. In maths, for example, you might eventually get to the point where you are interleaving questions on multiplying fractions, dividing fractions, adding fractions and subtracting fractions. But actually, if you did that with pupils straight away, they would probably just get really confused. In that situation, you might block-practise first but then interleave once pupils have reached a decent level of knowledge. In a PE lesson, doing badminton and learning different shots, instead of practising lots of smash shots and then lots of drop shots, we would interleave them – we'd mix them all up.

Principle 5: spaced retrieval practice prevents forgetting

This is the last principle from me, which combines the 'spacing effect' with the 'retrieval practice effect': retrieval practice should be spaced. Retrieval practice is a really common practice in all of our schools now. It's where we are getting pupils to revisit and remember content that they have learned previously, whether that be knowledge or skills. Spaced practice is where instead of doing massed practice on something and then never coming back to it, we do a bit when we first learn it and then come back to this after a delay, and so on. We know that spaced practice is effective because it prevents forgetting as every time we revisit a topic, we forget less and we forget more slowly.

What we want to do is combine those two things. We want to do retrieval practice, but we want to make sure it is spread out over time. So, we might do our initial learning and the next day or the next lesson we might do some retrieval practice on that content. Then, try to revisit that again a couple of weeks later, and then maybe a month later, and then maybe a term later, so that we're constantly revisiting. One of the reasons why that is super effective is because of the way in which our memories are made up. Each memory essentially has a storage strength and a retrieval strength. Storage strength is how well stored something is in your long-term memory, how well learned something actually is. Retrieval strength is how easily you can bring it to mind.

When we first learn something, it will have a really high retrieval strength. We just learned it, so we can recall it quite easily. But we'll have a low storage strength as it's not really well embedded in our long-term memory. What we've seen in research from Robert and Elizabeth Bjork is that if we allow retrieval strength to fade – meaning something is difficult to retrieve because we haven't done it recently – when we do manage to retrieve it, the increase in the storage strength – how well embedded it is in our long-term memory – is much bigger. What we're trying to do with spaced retrieval practice is allow the retrieval strength to fade, so that we can then increase the storage strength by much more when it is retrieved. That is why retrieval practice should be spaced.

Retrieval practice in practice

There are a few other things we might want to bear in mind when we're doing retrieval practice to make sure it is most effective. The first sounds really simple, but it is that **review should concentrate on the most important aspects of a topic**. We can't review every single thing that we've taught because we don't have the time, so we need to think about the most important things that your pupils need to know and be able to do, and make sure your retrieval practice concentrates on that.

Also, **the format of the review should match both the pupils and the subject**. We often see quiz questions being done with subjects like art or PE, when actually it might be better to ask pupils to practise skills through their retrieval practice, for example, rather than answering written questions. We know that retrieval practice for our youngest students will have to be verbal. It may be a lot of matching exercises or doing things with other adults, but obviously that will be different for older pupils.

Retrieval should include both factual and higher-order knowledge. We often see retrieval practice as just being a recall of factual content, when, actually, we now know from research that if we want to improve our pupils' abilities to perform higher-order skills like analysis, evaluation, comparison, etc. from memory, eventually our retrieval practice also needs to include those things. Whatever greater depth or really challenging tasks look like in your year group or subject, we also need to include those in our retrieval practice and be getting pupils to do them from memory as well as just answering factual questions.

Retrieval and reviews must provide the appropriate level of difficulty. We want them to be challenging enough so they make us process the material, but not so difficult that pupils fail them.

Any revisiting should be low stakes. We know that retrieval practice is most effective when we're not collecting scores and not using it to assess learning. The goal of retrieval practice should remain to help pupils remember more next time, not to judge what they remember now.

Finally, research shows, especially with our youngest pupils, that it is really important to **provide corrective feedback**. We know we've got limited time, but especially on those questions that pupils didn't answer correctly, we need to make sure that when they've done the retrieval practice, we're providing feedback on that.

Questions

John Tomsett (JT): How do storytelling and using hinterland knowledge fit in with cognitive load limits in the working memory?

Jade Pearce (JP): Yes, great question. What we know is that when we've learned something and it is in our long-term memory, we can think about it without it causing as much cognitive load. Essentially, we still want to share stories, hinterland knowledge, etc. with our pupils, but we want to do so when they've already put the basics into their long-term memory. In other words, we don't do it all at the start.

JT: Does the research show what the rough effect sizes are if these strategies are incorporated into classrooms?

JP: The effect sizes will differ between different strategies. Interleaving, for example, might be different to retrieval practice, so there isn't one answer to that. In theory, these effects should have really big impacts on student learning. And certainly when I've introduced these as a teacher, as a head of department and then in a whole-school setting, and it's made a positive impact on outcomes.

JT: Why do you think there is pushback against this cognitive-science-based theory of teaching and learning?

JP: There are two criticisms or pushbacks that I hear. The first is that it is too formulaic, as in: we all have to do retrieval practice at the start of every lesson and it has to be five questions. I would say that's probably a result of poor execution from leaders who are trying their best to achieve some consistency and ensure that everyone is implementing these practices, which we know are really important for our pupils. They are probably doing it in a tightly controlled way, which leads to pushback from teachers at their school.

The second thing I hear is that it's common sense: 'We've always done retrieval practice.' 'Of course, we do retrieval practice all the time.'

Actually, we do question our students all the time, for example, and that's retrieval practice. But I would say, how consistent is it? How refined is it? And how systematic is it? Have you identified the most important knowledge that you're going to retrieve? Do you have a retrieval practice curriculum where you know you're going to revisit that knowledge a certain number of times?

Those are the kinds of pushbacks I feel exist, but I certainly think the benefits outweigh any concerns we might have.

JT: What about the language we use when discussing the cognitive theories, like 'processing', 'coding', 'retrieval', 'storage'? It makes it sound as if we're computers, and we're not. Have you got any thoughts about that?

JP: In terms of the language that we use, I do agree. And you hear really great comments from people like Greg Ashman on Twitter who will say the whole cognitive load/explicit instruction/cognitive science model of memory says we do not learn like a computer. It's not that once you put something in, it stays there forever, etc. So, it may be worth reflecting on the language used to see if we could find more appropriate alternatives.

JT: Do we have a sense of where emotions fit into learning?

JP: That's a really interesting question. I've just recently read a paper that looked at the impact of emotions on cognitive load. It showed that any heightened emotions, whether that be excitement or anxiety, cause cognitive load and take up space in our working memory, and therefore can reduce the capacity we have to concentrate on learning. That's only one snippet of it. I've had really great discussions with other people about the fact that classrooms and learning aren't just a scientific process. They are social, they are collaborative, etc. So, we probably need more discussion of that alongside cognitive science.

Chapter 17
Leadership 55 wisdom – the buck stops with you

Managing the fact that the buck stops with you

The first time the buck stopped with me, it came as a bit of a surprise. It was late August 2003, a week before I began as headteacher at Lady Lumley's School, when the deputy told me we didn't have a psychology teacher for the start of term. My first thought was 'Why is he telling me?' And then it suddenly struck me that, ultimately, it was my job to ensure we were fully staffed.

The thing is no one forces you to become a headteacher. If you have chosen that career path, you need to have secure coping strategies in order to survive in the role. You certainly have to be able to control your thinking. The mantra I try to live by is from Shakespeare's *Hamlet*: 'Nothing is either good or bad but thinking makes it so.'

An appreciation of one's own insignificance is, generally, a good thing. There are 32,000 schools in the UK and between 2 and 5 million schools in the world, depending on how you define a school; as a headteacher, you lead just one of them. Keeping things in perspective, but not too wide a perspective, is an important facet of running a school and leading a contented life. Certain things have to matter, but not too much. If you find yourself taking yourself too seriously, go and scrape some chewing gum off the carpet in the school reception. Or take a walk around your local cemetery…we are all going to die one day.

On occasion, I respond to situations inappropriately. I once broke down hopelessly at a colleague's packed funeral and people couldn't look me in the eye at the wake. For them it must have been deeply unsettling, like when you see your dad cry for the first time. Colleagues need to feel they are in safe hands, especially when there is such uncertainty and fear in our professional world. You have to hold steady.

So, here are my top six tips for early career headteachers for managing the fact that the buck stops with you:

1. **Shun self-pity.** Recently I was asked which human characteristic I most despised and I replied, 'self-pity'. When things go awry, I never ask, 'Why me?' Rather, I ask, 'Why not me?' Once you accept that being human means you will suffer pain, life becomes significantly easier.

2. **When things go wrong in school, learn to step back and laugh at your predicaments.** You can choose to train your brain that way. As Frankl says in his life-affirming treatise *Man's Search for Meaning*: 'Everything can be taken from a man but one thing: the last of the human freedoms—to choose one's attitude in any given set of circumstances, to choose one's own way.' Take a helicopter view of life. In a week, a month, six months, a year, what appears a huge issue now will seem a mere trifling inconvenience.

3. **Get a good night's sleep.** I once heard Stella Rimington, erstwhile director general of MI5, say that the only advice she could give to headteachers is to get a good night's sleep. She thought it impossible

to make sound decisions when you are fatigued. And when it comes to sleeping, invest heavily in the best mattress for your bed you can find. Seriously!

4. **Remember that every single challenge that you have faced until this point in your life, you have met.** No matter what life has thrown at you, you are here now, you have endured. When we have an unexpected fire alarm, I stand in the centre of the playground, as 1700 people mass around me, and I tell myself that this too shall pass. It really helps. Especially if it is raining.

5. When you find yourself in the eye of the storm, when the crisis you are dealing with tests you to the limit, when the buck has not just stopped with you, but has sat with all its crushing weight upon your chest so you can hardly breathe, **remember that you only have to deal with the next 60 seconds**. And once you have survived those 60 seconds, you can cope with the next 60, and then the next. One. Minute. At. A. Time.

6. Finally, to survive in the job and develop into an effective headteacher, you have to hold two utterly contradictory notions in your head, simultaneously, and hold them in balance, with a commitment to do a good job, but not in a way that will cost you your family or your health. The first notion is that this job of headteacher really matters. These kids really matter. They get one go at this education thing and we have a moral responsibility to do our very best for them. The second is that what we do in our careers doesn't matter at all. You get to the end of it and wonder what all the fuss was about. You were there, and then you're gone. 'What was his name? Tom? Or was it John? You know, grey hair, big nose. I think he was head here once…'

Chapter 18
A conversation on unpacking oracy with Clare Sealy

This is about unpacking oracy. Now, one of my big things about what happens in education is that things become trendy. And then people do mad things because they don't really understand them. I think oracy has so much that is good about it. But I get slightly nervous because it's trendy, and people will start doing crazy things. So, this is meant to be an inoculation against craziness or, rather, helping us really understand oracy. The EEF's great materials on effective professional development suggest that in order to be effective, professional development needs to build knowledge, motivate teachers, develop teacher techniques and embed practice. If you do all of those, it's likely to go well, but if you miss out on one of those, then it won't be as effective.

I think, sometimes with oracy, people get excited about it and they don't understand what it can and can't do. If that knowledge building block isn't there, then we could be in a situation where we don't get the most out of it. While pupil and teacher motivation may be present, they may have misunderstood and misapplied initial knowledge. Hopefully, this will help prevent that from happening in your schools.

My big thing that I go on about all the time is that we can use oracy in two different ways. We can use it to learn *through* talk and we can use it to learn *how to* talk. The Oracy Commission have a third one, which is learning about talk. I'm putting that in with learning how to talk. So, learning through talk and learning how to talk. What they actually mean is learning through talk is pedagogy – using oracy as a pedagogical tool. Learning how to talk is looking at our curriculums and asking in which subjects, at what point, is learning how to talk really important.

Clearly, if you're teaching somebody French or Spanish, learning how to talk in that language is really important. If you're teaching drama, learning how to talk in dramatic ways is essential – that's what drama is about – learning certain ways of talking and how other people have used that. If you're an Early Years teacher, then language and communication is, after all, one of the prime areas of the curriculum.

Sometimes there's a curriculum reason why you're using talk and sometimes there's a pedagogical reason. Sometimes there's both. Things go wrong when we muddle the two up. The rationale is either the pedagogical reason – it supports high-quality, inclusive teaching – or it's a curriculum requirement, sometimes both. Being really clear about why you're using it means you're using it deliberately and thoughtfully. You need to understand why you've chosen to use oracy as opposed to writing, for example, or digital technology, or movement and gesture. Because all of these strategies are open to us, and every choice we make has an opportunity cost.

Opportunity cost is a term from economics. If we choose to do something, we are also choosing not to do other things. The things we're choosing not to do... Might they have been better? So, it's always worth asking: if we're going to use oracy, what's the opportunity cost? Is this the best tool for the job? Lots of times, the answer will be *yes*, but sometimes it won't be. If we get carried away with oracy being the latest trendy thing, we might end up using it just for the sake of it, thinking it must be good because it's oracy. If we're senior leaders and decide we want to see oracy in all lessons, without considering whether it's the right tool for the job in that lesson, then we might drive that inappropriately.

I'm labouring this point because it's very close to my heart. Pedagogy and curriculum do not serve oracy; oracy serves pedagogy and curriculum. That is my point number one.

Now, let's look at the ways we can learn through talk – how oracy can support pedagogy. It could be a choice we make within our pedagogy. There are probably more than this, but I'm going to talk about four main ways in which talk can really support teaching and learning. I'm focusing more on using talk as opposed to using listening, because I take it as read that we expect children to listen in lessons. So, the four things are *building belonging, checking for understanding*, something called the '*sea of write*', which I'll unpack a bit, and *thinking hard*. I'm going to unpack each one of those in turn.

Building belonging, particularly these days in a post-Covid environment, and in an environment where social media has taken children away from face-to-face communication, is crucial. Children these days play out a lot less and meet up face to face much less than they used to in their own time. So, fostering a feeling that you belong in school is really important. You've probably heard of Doug Lemov, of *Teach Like a Champion* fame. He's also written a book called *Reconnect: Building School Culture for Meaning, Purpose, and Belonging*. He talks about amplifying the signals of belonging, and using oracy is one way of doing that.

A benchmark from Voice 21 is that we should value every voice and hear every voice. The teacher supports all students to participate in, and benefit from, oracy in the classroom. The teacher listens meaningfully to students, encouraging them to develop their ideas further, and creates a culture in which students do the same.

So, one pedagogical reason for using oracy is that it builds belonging and creates a sense of being listened to.

A second reason, and this is very much a whistle-stop tour, is in terms of checking for understanding. In many Ofsted reports I've read, assessment comes up, and they don't mean summative assessment or statistical analysis. They mean teachers really knowing and assessing, usually in the moment, whether learning is happening or not. If it's not landing, then adjusting their teaching and responding dynamically to address those needs. That's what they mean. The way we do that is by checking as we go for understanding because learning is invisible. We can't see learning going on inside children's heads. We have to check, to draw it out, to make the invisible visible. If we don't do that, we get the 'conveyor belt curriculum', where the teacher carries on and on, and the curriculum just bypasses children. Some children just aren't getting it, particularly more vulnerable or disadvantaged children.

There are three primary ways we can check for understanding: through writing, showing or talking. Writing might involve a longer piece in a book, on the screen or on a mini-whiteboard. Showing might involve an indicator system – green or red cards, thumbs up or down, a number of fingers or a digital clicker. Talking could be one child addressing the whole class or talking to a partner while the teacher listens in. All of these are valid.

It's about teachers making good, informed, judicious choices about the right tool at the right time. Sometimes writing is better, sometimes showing is better and sometimes talking is better. What's the right tool for the right job? Writing in the moment, for example, works best for shorter answers – one word, a sentence or a calculation. A shorter answer, maybe on a whiteboard, can really help. Showing is great for yes/no answers, and talking is better for longer answers. It depends on what you're checking for, as to which tool you're going to use.

When we use talking to check for understanding, this is obvious but worth saying: as a teacher, you can either attend to one learner giving a longer answer or many learners giving short written, signalled or spoken answers. Both have their place, but it's about knowing what you're asking and which tool will work best.

So, we've talked about building belonging and checking for understanding. My third point may be less familiar: it's something I've called the 'language of write'. This is because the language we use when we write formally, or when we speak formally, is very different from conversational language. The sort of language I'm using with you now is different from conversational language. It uses a different idiom and complete sentences.

We primarily learn that formal language at school. You might learn it a bit at home through watching documentaries, the news, or similar, but generally, it's not conversational. It's nobody's natal tongue.

Writing is not transcribed speech. It uses sentences, not fragments. It's a new language for all of us. And the good thing about it, is it turbocharges the ability to think in abstract and analytical ways. There are cultures that are pre-literate – they still use abstract analytical thought, but much less so than in cultures where there is widespread literacy.

So, you might say, why am I talking about writing? It's because, as well as being able to write in those ways, we also need to be able to speak in those ways, using that sort of idiom. Sometimes schools have policies that, when you answer, it has to be in a full sentence. Then you might have people saying, 'Well, that's wrong, because conversationally, we don't use full sentences.' Both those people are right – conversationally, we don't. If children are doing what is sometimes called messy talk, as Douglas Barnes described it – exploratory talk when you're exploring ideas, or messy talk – and presentational talk, when you're presenting ideas more formally, then when we're doing that sort of presentational talk, it probably would be in full sentences. When you're doing exploratory talk, it may not be, and forcing children to speak in full sentences too early when they're exploring their thoughts can hamper them.

Sometimes we can use exploratory talk to move from that messy stage into the more formal stage, but not always. Here's a representation of that. We might have spontaneous social interaction, which will definitely not be in sentences. Then we might do some exploratory talk, exploring an idea with a partner or in a group of three or so. Maybe we'll have some jottings on a whiteboard that we can revise as we recast our thoughts and try to recast them into formal academic idiom.

Sometimes you don't do that. Sometimes it's enough to just explore ideas, and it doesn't need to be put into formal academic idiom. It depends on the age of the children you're teaching and it depends on the subject. For example, if you were in a PE lesson and wanted people to come up with a definition for 'agility', it may stay at the exploratory stage and not get into presentation. Talking of agility, here's an example. If we said, 'Hey, could you define agility?' – something that secondary PE teachers might ask children because it's one of the characteristics of fitness – in a conversational stage, children might say something like, 'Yeah, agility, yeah, it's like when you move quickly, like when you dodge and feint and stuff.' If you said, 'Right, take your initial ideas, and let's work them up a bit and come up with that in a full sentence,' they might use their initial thoughts and say, 'Agility is when you can move position quickly.' If you said, 'Yes, but we want that in really formal academic English,' it might then become: 'Agility is the ability to change the position of the body quickly and control the movement.' You see the way it moves through the spectrum there.

If we unpack that, how do they look different? In the conversational social idiom, it's not full sentences – it's fragments. There are voice hesitations, the ums and the ahs, and informal discourse markers like 'so', 'like' and 'you know when'. Those sorts of things are completely appropriate in that context. They're not bad; they're context-specific.

Then, in the exploratory talk, we're moving towards full sentences, but not insisting on them too early. We're importing technical vocabulary and taking out those 'likes', 'so' and 'you know when' – removing those informal discourse markers. If we want to move it up to the presentational stage, that's when we're taking the sentence and really polishing it, maybe using some nominalisation, such as turning verbs into nouns, and perhaps making it less personal, replacing 'you' with forms that don't need that.

That's what I call the 'sea of write'. The reason I've called it the 'sea of write' is because of the famous James Britton quotation: 'Writing floats on a sea of talk.' That's true, but I've inverted it: sometimes talk floats on a sea of writing. Unless we learn to speak in the ways and use the idiom that writing uses, we won't be able to speak formally in a presentational sense. Of course, we'll be able to talk in other ways.

Right, the last one on pedagogy is externalising our thinking. Obviously, our thinking is invisible, but it's invisible to us, too. One way that we can help content be really learned and understood by students is by giving them tools to expand and externalise their thinking. Take it out of their brains, if you like, and look at it. That enables them to expand ideas, integrate it with prior knowledge and organise their ideas for meaning.

There are four tools we could use to do this. We could use exploratory talk – that messy talk. We could use writing. We could create visuals, such as a graphic organiser or a flow diagram. Or it could be through enacting, like using Dienes apparatus in maths to model a problem, manipulatives in maths or similar tools. So, we have four different ways to externalise thinking, and talk is one of those, which takes us back to thinking about the right tool for the job. It won't always be talk, but sometimes it really will be. This is why building knowledge is so important: so that teachers can make judicious choices about the right tool for the right job.

Okay, that's my whistle-stop tour of oracy as pedagogy. Now, oracy as curriculum. The oracy framework from Voice 21 and Oracy Cambridge talks about oracy comprising physical, linguistic, cognitive and social-emotional aspects. I just want you to pay attention to the physical and social-emotional aspects and ask yourself: where in your school day, or in your school week, in your curriculum, do children get taught how to speak physically and how to talk socially and emotionally? There is no one answer. In some primary schools, that might come in through PSHE, it might come in through drama, or some schools might have an oracy lesson as a timetabled activity. It might come in through English, or it might be a mix of those. In secondary schools, it's similar – they might have more discrete drama time, for example. But it's asking yourself the question: where do these get explicitly taught in my school? Because they do need to be explicitly taught, and that's a curriculum issue. It's not a pedagogical issue. Once they know how to do it, then they can use it. But initially, it's a curriculum issue.

And then the other thing – and again, this is so brief and so whistle-stoppy – is to really bear in mind that subjects are different, and therefore the place of oracy within a curriculum is different. For example, as I said before, in MFL (French, Spanish, German, whatever), clearly you are going to use speaking and listening. Those are curriculum objectives of those subjects. If you think about history, not so much – maybe not quite as much, although definitely to a degree, yes. But let's unpack that quickly.

We can think about subjects as having a mission or a quest. We can think about some subjects having a mainly descriptive quest – describing the world as it is. Some have more of an interpretive quest, like making interpretations of the world. Some have a more expressive quest, expressing truth or meaning. And some have a problem-solving quest. Now, this is a massive simplification because subjects straddle these quests, but bear with me just for our purposes. Now, we can say that, in the main, maths, science, some aspects of English and physical geography have a more descriptive quest. Human geography, history, RE and English have a more interpretive quest. Expressive quests are more for the arts and some aspects of English. And then problem-solving quests include things like computing, D&T, and food and nutrition. This is a massive oversimplification – it's much more complicated than that.

But bear that in mind. In a descriptive subject – or, I should say, descriptive quest, not so much a subject – the community of scholars that follows that subject has a single truth as an aspiration. So, if you're a scientist and you want to describe force, the scientific community has a single truth that force equals mass times acceleration. It's not like, 'Well, I think it's mass times acceleration squared.' That's not how it works. It's force equals mass times acceleration – causal science.

In an interpretive quest, such as history, geography or aspects of RE, excellent answers are contested within the academic community. That's part of learning that subject: to know that truths are very much contested. And that's part of what we do as a historian, geographer or scholar of RE. In expressive subjects, there are many right answers. There is no single truth about the meaning of *Macbeth* or whatever. In problem-solving subjects, the question is: does it work?

Within that, giving an opinion is sometimes seen by people as the holy grail of oracy. It's part of oracy, but it's only a part, and it fits better into when we're being interpretive or expressive. That's when giving an opinion really earns its stripes. Because yes, as a historian, I do need to give an opinion about what the causes of World War I were, for example, if that's what I'm studying. That's what historians do. But it's an informed opinion based on sources, not just, 'Well, I think.' We do need to do that, and using oracy is a good way of doing that.

Again, in English, if I'm reading a poem and analysing it or looking at a piece of art, there are many right answers. Using oracy as a way of garnering and exploring opinions is really important. It's not that it's never used when we're being descriptive or problem solving, but it's used a lot less. In maths, for example, you would use it when you're generalising or formulating proofs, but there are lots of times when you wouldn't use it. So a blanket 'Everyone's got to be using oracy all the time in their subjects' doesn't always honour the rationale behind those subjects.

That's me finished on that – just doing a bit of a plug, you know, like when they have chat shows: 'Hey, read the book!' If you're a primary practitioner, or maybe even if you aren't, I've written a chapter on oracy in *The researchED Guide to Primary Literacy*, which is just out. I've also written two blogs, one called 'Oracies not oracy', which is the same thing I've just talked about today but a bit longer. And then the other one, 'Understanding oracy, understanding writing', expands on that whole 'sea of write' idea.

Questions

John Tomsett (JT): I did some work on oracy with a group of schools in the West Midlands quite recently. They were talking about the local idiom and I was talking about one of the people on Geoff Barton's commission. He has pretty trenchant views about rejecting the hegemony of the traditional King's English and promoting the importance of local idiom.

Clare Sealy (CS): I think that's important. Local idiom is really fundamental to our sense of personal identity and should be nurtured, cherished and respected. But it's about teaching our children – and of course, it depends on the age of the child. What you would say to a 15-year-old and what you'd say to a 3-year-old are fundamentally different, with 8-year-olds somewhere in the middle. What we want is for all our children to be able to operate and be valued and respected in their own idiom, whatever that is, but also to be able to, where necessary, code-switch into using the more formal standardised forms of spoken and written English when it's appropriate to do so – not because their own dialect is inferior. It's just context-specific. The whole point about having standardised forms of speaking and writing is that they're standardised so people beyond the local can understand them, and you can communicate more widely. That's why, for instance, with a 3-year-old in nursery or a 5-year-old, it's less important for them right then. But as they get older, we want them to inhabit, and feel that they belong in, an academic space and can communicate beyond the immediate bubble – that is, their family, their school, their class – but to be able to communicate with the world at large. To do that, they need to communicate in forms that are more standardised.

Some of us are born with the advantage that our local idiom is the same as, or very similar to, the standardised form. Well, lucky for us. But that's not the case for everyone. I completely understand who you're talking about and I think, funnily enough, he doesn't tend to write in local idiom, though, does he?

JT: So does this impact people not having that tool?

CS: That's learning about talk, but you also need to be able to use it. My whole 'sea of write' piece is really about that. It's about enabling children to become fluent in this language that, in a way, none of us speak at home. Even if you're RP (received pronunciation), that's just not what we do. We learn that at school, and we need to have it scaffolded, modelled for us, and structured so that we can do that.

JT: What advice would you give teachers to avoid the lethal mutations of oracy?

CS: I think this is about building capacity and having those conversations about when this works. Like with loads of things in education: when does this work and when does this not work? When would this be a really bad idea? This thing is a really good idea, but when would it be a really bad idea to use it? Always bring it back to 'Why are we doing this?' And not just 'Why?' – it's 'Why are we doing it now, in this particular context? Why have you made this choice? What have we chosen not to do? And how can we defend why this choice is better than that choice?'

JT: If you were beginning to develop pupils' oracy skills in your school, how would you prioritise?

CS: I think I'd start off with the pedagogical side of it rather than the curriculum side of it. Obviously, if you're teaching Early Years, then you have to have language and communication. But, generally, I think I'd work on the pedagogical side. I probably would work on things like externalising your thinking. Oracy is a way of externalising your thinking. Because also, then, you're just really talking about how to externalise thoughts, with oracy as one tool. But we can also think about other tools. Maybe the checking for understanding, because that often doesn't happen. Teachers may check for understanding, but whether they do anything as a result is another matter. So I think I'd settle on those two.

If you do that, then you will be building belonging anyway. Maybe the whole 'sea of write' sentence-based idiom stuff comes further along the path. But I think I'd stick with those two to start with.

JT: That's great. Was there anything you'd want to say or reflect on about Geoff's oracy commission and their findings?

CS: No, I think, in general, it's a sensible piece. I like the way they are nuanced about it and try not to say, 'Yay, you must do this! It's the latest thing.' They're being sensible about it. They question whether we need to have an oracy curriculum. That's something I know Voice 21 really advocates, but I'm a bit wary of that. I think we should think about pedagogy and oracy. We need to look at our curriculums and think about where oracy fits into them, rather than saying, 'Here's an oracy curriculum.' So, yeah, I think it's a sensible piece.

JT: Thanks, Clare. That's been hugely helpful.